KARANIS

An Egyptian Town in Roman Times

DISCOVERIES OF THE UNIVERSITY OF MICHIGAN EXPEDITION TO EGYPT
(1924–1935)

T0152059

edited by
Elaine K. Gazda

with a new preface and updated bibliography by
T. G. Wilfong

Kelsey Museum Publication 1

Kelsey Museum of Archaeology
University of Michigan
2004

This is the first in a new series, Kelsey Museum Publications (KMP), from the Kelsey Museum of Archaeology at the University of Michigan. KMP will embrace a wide range of publications: exhibition catalogues, gallery guides, semi-popular presentations of particular types of material in the Kelsey Museum, studies of material from its past excavations, selections from its rich photographic archives, and papers from conferences and workshops held under Kelsey sponsorship. The initial titles in the series include:

KMP 1, 2004   *Karanis, An Egyptian Town in Roman Times: Discoveries of the University of Michigan Expedition to Egypt (1924–1935)*, edited by Elaine K. Gazda (2nd ed., with a new preface and updated bibliography by T. G. Wilfong).

KMP 2, 2004   *Prehistorians Round the Pond: Reflections on Aegean Prehistory as a Discipline. Papers Presented at a Workshop Held in the Kelsey Museum of Archaeology, March 14–16, 2003*, edited by John F. Cherry, Despina Margomenou, and Lauren E. Talalay.

KMP 3, 2005   *This Fertile Land: Signs + Symbols in the Early Arts of Iran and Iraq*, edited by Margaret Cool Root.

On the cover: View of Karanis, the "House of the Banker" (Kelsey Museum Archives, 5.4235).

ISBN: 0-9741873-0-5

TABLE OF CONTENTS

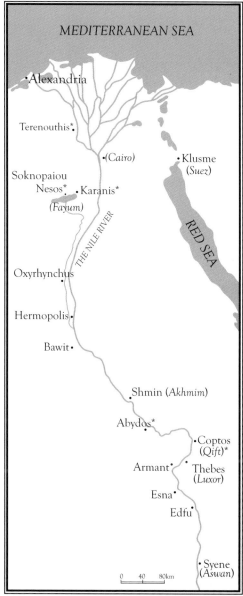

Fig. 1. Egypt in the Roman period (modern place names in italics; sites of University of Michigan fieldwork in Egypt, past and present, indicated with asterisk).

PREFACE TO THE SECOND EDITION

Just over twenty years ago, the Kelsey Museum of Archaeology published the original edition of the book you now hold in your hands—*Karanis: An Egyptian Town in Roman Times*, by Elaine K. Gazda, then Associate Director of the museum. This book was originally prepared to accompany an exhibition of the same name, on display at the Kelsey Museum in Ann Arbor from March 12 to June 26, 1983. After the exhibition closed, however, the book continued to be available and took on a life of its own. It gradually became widely known outside the Kelsey Museum's local audience as an essential guide to the site of Karanis and the University of Michigan excavations there. This book can lay claim to being one of the Kelsey Museum's "best sellers," but the first edition finally sold out in early 2004. The present reprint is intended primarily to bring one of our best-known publications back into print; it retains the format and text of the 1983 book and most of the illustrations (although these have been newly scanned from original archival copies or negatives where possible). In reprinting the earlier book, however, we have also highlighted the more recent and ongoing activity relating to the Kelsey Museum's Karanis material through a new preface and an updated bibliography.

Karanis was a town in Egypt's Fayum region, founded around 250 BC to house a population meant to work newly reclaimed agricultural land. It was a farming community with a diverse population and a complex material culture that lasted for hundreds of years after its foundation. Ultimately abandoned by its inhabitants and partly covered by the encroaching desert, Karanis eventually proved to be an extraordinarily rich archaeological site, yielding thousands of artifacts and texts on papyrus that provide a wealth of information about daily life in the Roman period Egyptian town. The University of Michigan excavated at Karanis between 1924 and 1935, and during these seasons the Egyptian government granted nearly 45,000 of the artifacts discovered to the University of Michigan. Along with extensive archival records and photographs of the excavation, the Karanis material forms one of the major components of the collection of the Kelsey Museum of Archaeology.

Karanis: An Egyptian Town in Roman Times tells of the history and culture of Karanis and also provides a useful introduction to the University of Michigan excavations. It represents the state of research into Karanis at Michigan in 1983, a time of renewed interest in the site and the University of Michigan's work there. Indeed, the book and the exhibition followed on a series of significant publications about the site: major works by Louise Shier, Barbara Johnson and Elinor Husselman had appeared only a few years earlier, publishing (respectively) the lamps, the pottery and the topography and architecture of the later seasons of excavation. Karanis material had also figured prominently in a number of Kelsey Museum exhibitions in the years just before 1983: "Gods of Egypt in the Graeco-Roman Period" (1977), "The Art of the Ancient Weaver: Textiles from Egypt (4th–12th century AD)" (1980), "Wondrous Glass: Reflections on the World of Rome" (1982) and Elaine Gazda's own earlier exhibition "Guardians of the Nile: Sculptures from Karanis in the Fayum (c. 250 BC–AD 450)" (1978). Outside of Ann Arbor, interest in the site of Karanis had grown as well, with excavations by Egyptian and French projects and a magnetometric survey of the site in the 1970s and '80s, while papyrologists continued to publish and study documents from the site. Elaine Gazda's 1983 exhibition and publication appeared almost as a culmination of this wave of Karanis-related activity but also inspired new research and interest.

Since the publication of the original edition of the present book, much new research and activity on Karanis has taken place at Michigan and beyond. Karanis artifacts formed the basis for two substantial doctoral dissertations at Michigan following on the 1983 exhibition (Allen, 1985 and Higashi, 1990), while Karanis material in general continued to be used for wider thematic exhibitions at the Kelsey Museum (note especially "The Beginning of Understanding: Writing in the Ancient World," for which see Allen and Dix, 1991). Kelsey Museum Karanis artifacts featured prominently in two important traveling exhibitions and their catalogues—"Beyond the Pharaohs" (Auth, 1989) and "Art and Holy Powers" (Maguire et al., 1989)—that did much to expose this material to a wider audience.

The documents on papyrus from Karanis have continued to occupy the attention of papyrologists, and the University of Michigan has been a center for this research, thanks in large part to the efforts of Traianos Gagos, Archivist of the University of

Michigan Papyrus Collection, to maintain and promote not only the papyri but also a fully equipped papyrological library and study center. The early 1990s saw a substantial move at the University of Michigan, initiated by Traianos Gagos and Peter van Minnen, to recontextualize the Karanis papyri in the archaeology of the site (resulting in such work as Gagos, 2001 and van Minnen, 1994). The papyri from Karanis at Michigan and elsewhere are rapidly becoming part of a worldwide effort to publish papyri online, the Advanced Papyrological Information System (APIS) project; Karanis papyri at Michigan can be accessed via the website of the University of Michigan Papyrus Collection at: http://www.lib.umich.edu/pap/ (this website also contains a wealth of information and resources relating to papyri in general). The complex relation between papyri and other artifacts from the Karanis excavations continues to be a focus at Michigan, as seen in the Kelsey Museum exhibition "Digging up a Story: The House of Claudius Tiberianus," which arose from a student project to place a papyrus archive into its archaeological context.

At the Kelsey Museum of Archaeology today, the Karanis material remains at the heart of our research and educational outreach programs. Thousands of students and visitors annually encounter Karanis through our permanent installation, while others get even closer views, through exposure in seminars and university courses, special tours and our Educational Outreach program's "Karanis Daily Life Kit" (a selection of artifacts presented by museum docents to tour groups). The Kelsey Museum's permanent installation of Karanis material, which currently includes a reconstructed Karanis house context curated by Janet Richards, will soon take on a new look, as we prepare for an expanded exhibit space in our new wing, thanks to a major donation by Edwin and Mary Meader. Material from the Karanis excavations has formed a significant component of several recent thematic exhibitions at the Kelsey Museum: the student-curated "Caught Looking: Excavating the Kelsey" (1996), "A Taste of the Ancient World" (1996–97), "Animals in the Kelsey!" (2000) and the faculty-curated "Byzantium" (1994), "Women and Gender in Ancient Egypt" (1997), "Music in Roman Egypt" (1999), "The Fabric of Everyday Life: Textiles from Karanis, Egypt" (2001), "Individual and Society in Ancient Egypt" (2002) and "Archaeologies of Childhood: The First Years of Life in Roman Egypt" (2003–04), most with publications or websites either currently available or in preparation. These exhibitions are the result of ongoing curatorial research projects on the Karanis material, which include Thelma Thomas's current Karanis Textile Project (see Thomas, 2001–03), my own work on the music-related artifacts, toys, and exploration of different aspects of Karanis contexts along with projects to publish writing-related artifacts, Karanis sculpture and wall paintings (among many other groups of material), as well as the exploration of making Karanis artifacts and excavation records available to researchers online via the Kelsey Museum's website at http://www.lsa.umich.edu/kelsey (this URL provides access to all Kelsey Museum online exhibitions and activities).

Karanis material is an integral part of teaching and research for University of Michigan professors and students in a variety of programs (including the Interdepartmental Program in Classical Art and Archaeology, which is housed in the Kelsey Museum building, the departments of History of Art, Classical Studies, Near Eastern Studies, Anthropology and History, the Museum Studies Program and other units within the College of Literature, Science, and the Arts and the Rackham School of Graduate Studies), and curators Lauren Talalay and Susan Alcock have been instrumental in promoting student interest in Karanis. Students regularly do advanced research on the Kelsey Museum Karanis material: Michigan students are currently researching Karanis material relating to glass production, papyrus archives, magic, childhood and seal impressions, while recent undergraduate papers on Karanis domestic religion, panel and wall paintings, hieroglyphic inscriptions and other topics have already made valuable contributions to our knowledge of this material (a selection of student work on Karanis material will be published in *The Bulletin of the University of Michigan Museums of Art and Archaeology*, volume 15 [2004–05]).

Beyond Ann Arbor, the Kelsey Museum Karanis material has continued to be central to research on Graeco-Roman and late antique Egypt. Indeed, it is impossible to give a comprehensive listing of publications that illustrate or use artifacts or archival images from the Michigan excavations within the limits of this preface. A quick survey of some of the more important books in recent years to use

Karanis material, however, may give an impression of the ongoing importance of the Kelsey Museum Karanis holdings. Material from Karanis features prominently in the two most important English language surveys of Egypt in the later periods: Alan K. Bowman's *Egypt after the Pharaohs* (1986, 1996) and Roger S. Bagnall's *Egypt in Late Antiquity* (1993). Important recent thematic studies likewise make extensive use of Karanis artifacts and archival material at the Kelsey Museum, Richard Alston's recent monographs *Soldier and Society in Roman Egypt* (1995) and *The City in Roman and Byzantine Egypt* (2002) being good examples. The Karanis remains are especially important for social history, as can be seen in Jane Rowlandson's *Women and Society in Greek and Roman Egypt* (1998), and religion, seen in David Frankfurter's *Religion in Roman Egypt: Assimilation and Resistance* (1998). The archaeology of Karanis continues to excite much interest, vividly illustrated in Paola Davoli's recent survey of the archaeology of Karanis and other Fayum sites (1998). Scholarly interest has begun to coalesce around the latest material from Karanis; the traditional date for the abandonment of Karanis in the second half of the fifth century AD (the evidence for which is summarized in van Minnen, 1995) has begun to be challenged on the basis of both archaeological and textual evidence for later habitation (see Pollard, 1998 and Keenan, 2003), and the Kelsey Museum Karanis material is crucial for this ongoing discussion. Excavation and survey in the Fayum at sites relating to Karanis, including the fieldwork projects of Paola Davoli (University of Lecce) and Willeke Wendrich (heading a UCLA/Rijksuniversitiet Groningen project), promise much comparative data for the Karanis material, essential for future study. Clearly the reprint of Elaine Gazda's book comes at an exciting time for Karanis research.

Since the first edition of this book was my own introduction to Karanis and the Kelsey Museum of Archaeology back in 1985, it is a special pleasure for me to be writing a preface to its reprint. At that time I little suspected that I would eventually end up in Ann Arbor working at the Kelsey Museum on this very material. All of Elaine Gazda's acknowledgments from the original edition still hold true, and I would like to add a few more for this reprint. Specifically, I would like to thank Kelsey Museum curators Lauren Talalay for initiating discussion of this reprint, John Cherry for encouraging and seeing it through as part of our new publication series, Janet Richards for ongoing help, and Sharon Herbert for her support for this project and my work on the Kelsey Museum Karanis material. The text for the reprint comes from an interim online version of the original book (incorporating errata), which was prepared by Kirsten Firminger (as part of her project for me through the University of Michigan's Undergraduate Research Opportunity Program). Formatting and design of the reprint were done by Kelsey Museum editor Peg Lourie, based on the original layout of the 1983 edition. Curator of Slides and Photographs Robin Meador-Woodruff and Coordinator of Museum Collections Sebastián Encina performed the huge task of tracking down negatives for all the images and caption information, and Robin was also a great source of information and help in giving me an understanding of context of the original publication and subsequent events. I am grateful to Traianos Gagos for his encouragement of my own work and his facilitation of cooperation between the Kelsey Museum and the Papyrology Collection of the University Library, plus permission to publish illustrations of material in his keeping. Most of all, I would like to thank Elaine Gazda for her good-humored patience in the process of preparing this reprint, and for her continuing interest in my work on the Kelsey Museum Karanis material.

T. G. Wilfong
Associate Curator for Graeco-Roman Egypt, Kelsey Museum
Associate Professor of Egyptology, Department of Near Eastern Studies
August 2004

Fig. 2. The camp staff during Professor Kelsey's first visit to Karanis. Left to right: Enoch E. Peterson, H. Dunscombe Colt, Valeri Fausto, Harold Falconer, Joy Fletcher-Allen, Francis W. Kelsey, Byron Khun de Prorok, Edgar Fletcher-Allen, Edwin L. Swain (Kelsey Museum Archives, 5.2373).

ACKNOWLEDGMENTS FOR THE ORIGINAL EDITION

This catalogue and the exhibition it accompanies owe their genesis and realization to a host of individuals, both past and present. The contributions of those who played a central part in the discovery and scholarly elucidation of the town of Karanis and its inhabitants are noted in the first chapter. It seems fitting, however, to single out one of those persons here—Professor Francis W. Kelsey—to whom the tradition of research in Ancient Near Eastern and Classical Archaeology at The University of Michigan owes so great a debt. In the case of Karanis, it was due to his characteristic vision and enterprising spirit that the Kelsey Museum of Archaeology is in a position today to illustrate, in greater detail than any other museum outside of Egypt itself, what daily life was like in that extraordinary land in the Graeco-Roman period.

The richness of the Karanis collections housed on this campus has long been renowned among specialists all over the world. Rarely, however, have these collections been presented to the community at large in a manner which attempts to communicate the vitality of life in that ancient town. That the attempt has been made on this occasion is largely due to the interest, enthusiasm, and very hard work of two graduate students in the Interdepartmental Ph.D. Program in Classical Art and Archaeology—Andrea Berlin and Jacqueline Royer. A year ago they approached me about the possibility of preparing an exhibition as part of their program of graduate study, and soon thereafter the notion of focusing upon one of the major archaeological expeditions of The University of Michigan emerged. Their combined interests in fieldwork, architecture, and the Ancient Near East lent themselves ideally to the site of Karanis. These students have not only endured many unanticipated trials with remarkable cheer but at every stage of the project have contributed creatively and selflessly toward its successful outcome.

A complex undertaking of this sort would not be possible without the close cooperation of many members of the Museum staff. We are especially indebted to Director John Griffiths Pedley for his unfailing encouragement and support and to those members of the Kelsey staff who patiently forebore the many demands we made upon their energies, time and good will. En route from storage ranges to the galleries, the objects in the exhibition passed through the able hands of registrar Pamela Reister, conservator Amy Rosenberg, and photographers Fred Anderegg and Sue Webb. In the galleries they were placed in environments suggestive of their original settings ingeniously designed and artfully constructed by technician David Slee.

In the preparation of the catalogue, we have availed ourselves of the presence in Ann Arbor of numerous persons knowledgeable of the materials from Karanis: Professor Ludwig Koenen kindly offered bibliographical suggestions; Kelsey archivist Carol Finerman helped us locate documents pertaining to the history of the expedition; Ann van Rosevelt shared her expertise on textiles as did Marti Lu Allen on terracotta figurines and Louise Shier on lamps. The text of the catalogue has greatly benefited from the careful and perceptive reading of Assistant Curator Margaret Cool Root who guided us towards many refinements of both thought and prose. With administrative and stenographic efficiency, Kathleen Davis and Rachel Vargas saw us through numerous drafts of the catalogue text and exhibition labels as well as a myriad of other tasks which attend projects of this kind. Every detail of the production and design of the catalogue was overseen by Carol Hellman and Carol Gregg, respectively, of the University Publications staff. Finally, we are grateful to the College of Literature, Science and the Arts for a generous grant towards meeting publication and installation costs.

Elaine K. Gazda
Associate Director (in 1983)

Fig. 3. "House of the Banker" (C401/B501). The impressive stone entrance, unusual among the mud-brick houses of Karanis, is probably a sign of the proprietor's wealth. In the underground rooms of this house some 26,000 coins were found stored in jars and cloth bags (Kelsey Museum Archives, 5.4247).

KARANIS IN PERSPECTIVE

The town of Karanis occupies a unique place in the annals of Egyptian and Graeco-Roman archaeology. Although no more than a rustic agricultural village in the Fayum oasis, it looms large for us precisely because it provides a microcosm of life as it was lived by ordinary people in Egypt under Greek and Roman rule. The history of Karanis spans seven centuries, from the middle of the third century BC to the end of the fifth century AD. This was a period marked by momentous socioeconomic, political and religious change throughout the Mediterranean region—an era that saw not only the aftermath of the conquests of Alexander the Great but also the rise, dominion and eventual decline of Rome. To our understanding of these larger fluctuations in Hellenistic and Roman society Karanis contributes a specific point of reference which is documented in exceptional detail. The dry climate of Egypt has fostered the preservation of fragile material such as papyrus documents that have perished in other parts of the ancient world. Greek papyri, found in abundance at Graeco-Roman sites in Egypt, supply vast quantities of information on all aspects of daily life; but those that were found at Karanis have acquired a special significance. Thanks to the excavations of the town by The University of Michigan, these precious written documents can be read in the context of a full array of the material remains of the town in which they were written. Houses, temples, granaries and all that the inhabitants left in them over many generations of occupation lend a tangible reality to the events the papyri record.

The mound of Karanis rises conspicuously twelve meters above the surrounding plain, between the

Fig. 4. The mound of Karanis viewed from the cultivation at the south (Kelsey Museum Archives, 5.1663).

Royal Road from Cairo and an ancient irrigation canal. The plain itself lies along a limestone ridge which forms the northeastern rim of Egypt's fertile lake district, known as the Fayum. The nearby farming town of Kom Aushim can be reached within a two-hour drive from Egypt's capital city some fifty miles to the northeast. Ease of access to Karanis undoubtedly favored its development as a prosper-

ous agricultural center in antiquity. In the present century this accessibility favored the town's exploration as an archaeological site.

Discovery and Documentation

The first "excavations" carried on at Karanis were anything but scientific; in fact, they caused much

1

destruction of the site. As was common practice in Egypt in the late nineteenth and early twentieth century, local farmers obtained government permits to remove soil from the mound to use as fertilizer (sebbakh). Archaeological sites provided an excellent source of sebbakh because decomposed organic debris creates a soil very rich in nitrogen. The work of the sebbakhin at archaeological mounds did, however, have the effect of stimulating interest in the sites they dug; for in the course of their removal operations, ancient artifacts came to light and many of them found their way onto the antiquities market. Among the most common finds were papyri, which were soon coveted by both collectors and museums. These papyri inspired two English scholars to undertake the first serious archaeological work that had ever been done at Graeco-Roman sites in Egypt. In 1895 Bernard Pyne Grenfell and Arthur Surridge Hunt arrived in the northeastern Fayum with the intention of excavating for these valued documents.[1]

It was no coincidence that the first expedition of Grenfell and Hunt focused on the mound at Kom Aushim which they were able to identify, on the basis of the papyri they recovered there, as the site of ancient Karanis.[2] The mound, however, which had long been fertile ground for the local sebbakhin, appeared to them to have been "too hopelessly plundered to justify a long stay."[3] The following year they shifted their area of inquiry farther to the south, to Oxyrhynchus. Here Greek papyri "were harvested by the basketful." One sensational discovery—a leaf from a hitherto unknown work, Logia Iesu ("The Sayings of Our Lord")[4]—provided the impetus in 1897 for the Egypt Exploration Society in London to form a special Graeco-Roman branch, devoted primarily to the excavation and publication of papyri.[5]

Throughout the next two decades archaeological investigation at Graeco-Roman sites in Egypt continued to focus almost exclusively on the acquisition of these documents. Grenfell and Hunt described their approach to excavation as one which insured that other artifacts would be virtually ignored:

The method of digging for papyri in a town site presents some parallels to that of gold-mining. The gold-seeker follows a vein of quartz, while the papyrus-digger has to follow a stratum . . . of what the natives call afsh. . . . The gold-digger does not look for gold where there is no quartz, and similarly the papyrus-seeker may practically disregard any other kind of earth than afsh. Objects of stone, wood, or pottery he may find elsewhere, but without afsh he will hardly ever find papyrus.[6]

Archaeological excavations of Graeco-Roman sites remained tied largely to the pursuit of papyri well into the early 1920s. Meanwhile, at sites of Egypt's earlier and more renowned Dynastic period, archaeologists were working with a different end in mind—that of amassing a wide range of objects. In this they were pursuing a goal which had been established by Sir Flinders Petrie in a series of excavations between 1881 and 1891. For Petrie the aim of excavating was to supply "solidarity and reality . . . to what we only knew as yet on paper."[7] His great achievement lay in his recognition of the fact that objects, as well as papyri, are a type of historical evidence. As Petrie observed,

Most trivial things may be of value, as giving a clue to something else. Generally it is better to keep some examples of everything. . . . It need hardly be said that every subject should be attended to; the excavator's business is not to study his own speciality only, but to collect as much material as possible for the use of other students. To neglect the subjects that interest him less is not only a waste of his opportunities, but a waste of such archaeological material as may never be equaled again.[8]

Yet the objects which Petrie valued so highly were to a large extent seen by him and his contemporaries as ends in themselves, tokens of a past civilization.[9] It remained for others to appreciate the importance of the context in which they had been found.

Against the backdrop of this approach to the recording of antiquity, a new idea began to emerge. In 1920, Francis W. Kelsey, Professor of Latin Language and Literature, went to Egypt in order to acquire papyri for The University of Michigan. At Oxyrhynchus, in the company of B. P. Grenfell, he observed the material remains of Graeco-Roman sites in the process of destruction at the hands of the sebbakhin. Upon inquiring what arrangements had been made to record and interpret the archaeology of the sites, he was told that not only was no effort being expended to document the archaeological record but that previous work in Egypt had almost totally neglected the cultural background of the Graeco-Roman period in favor of that of the Dynastic era. Ultimately, Kelsey determined that an expedition must be organized and that "the obligation to fill so serious a gap in the knowledge of this important part of the Graeco-Roman world must rest upon Americans."[10]

Fig. 5. *Sebbakhin (fertilizer diggers) removing soil from the ancient mound of Karanis by rail car (Kelsey Museum Archives, 5.2465).*

Fig. 6. *Rolls of papyrus as found within the wooden threshold of a doorway in House 5026 (Kelsey Museum Archives, 5.1801).*

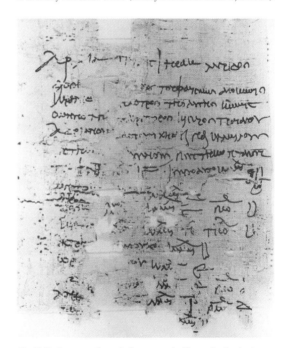

Fig. 7. *Declaration of camels that reports holdings of individual members of the guild of camelherds, AD 134–136 (P.Mich. inv. 5895 [= P. Mich. IX 543]). Reproduced with the permission of the Papyrology Collection, Graduate Library, The University of Michigan.*

In 1923 a grant from Horace H. Rackham enabled the newly formed Committee on Near East Research at The University of Michigan to plan trial excavations in Egypt. The search for a suitable site took place during the fall of 1924. On the first of November a team inspected the "hopelessly plundered" mound at Kom Aushim. Since the visit of Grenfell and Hunt the local *sebbakhin* had been continuously removing soil and in the intervening thirty years they had completely obliterated the center of the mound. Nevertheless their work had revealed large residential areas of the town which looked promising to the Michigan team. Permits were obtained, and work began in the first months of 1925.

Even in the first season, Karanis proved richer than had been anticipated both in the wealth of objects and the extent of the structures preserved. Inspired by this abundance of evidence, Professor Kelsey, in a memorandum to the Committee on Near East Research, stated the ambitious goals of the University's expedition. These were no less than

... the reconstruction of the environment of life in the Graeco-Roman period . . . [and the] increase of exact knowledge rather than the amassing of collections.[11]

It was inevitable that the concerns of the Michigan team would differ from those of previous excavators, both in the nature of the objects they considered worthwhile and the importance of the context in which those objects were found. Mirroring the interest in the totality of the environment even specimens of cereals, fruits and vegetables as well as mammalian and aquatic animal remains were

Fig. 8. Karanis excavations in progress; men and women from the village of Kom Aushim carry baskets of sand while clearing structures (Kelsey Museum Archives, 5.2741).

4

saved. Since earlier explorers of Egypt's past pursued other goals, the methods by which they had excavated were hardly applicable to the Karanis investigations. New, comprehensive recording techniques had to be developed to answer questions which had never before been asked.

A system was designed to enable the excavators to trace the evolution both of the town as a whole and of the individual structures within it. Prior to actual digging, the mound was surveyed and subdivided into seven large areas; and upon each area a grid of squares thirty-five meters to a side was superimposed. Within this framework plans and sections of the site were drawn. As excavation proceeded five discrete levels of occupation were distinguished—the uppermost and most recent was designated Level A, and letters B through E were assigned as earlier levels were identified. For each of the levels in the seven areas, plans and long sections were made. As a result, the structures throughout the site could be traced in detail; the superimposition of houses and any subsequent modifications could be seen.

Within every occupation level each house was explored room by room. The excavators kept notebooks of progress in the field, recording finds and observations as they occurred. Each artifact, as it was found, was identified by a label designating its level, house and room and was assigned a permanent number in the camp registry. On occasion, experts in the conservation of archaeological materials were consulted in an effort to provide appropriate care and treatment for the excavated finds. Detailed photographs were taken of every house

and group of artifacts as they were excavated layer by layer. In addition, movies were filmed of excavations in progress; these alone provided thousands of images of the city as it came to light.

The University of Michigan's excavations at Karanis marked a turning point in the study and exploration of Graeco-Roman Egypt; and their importance for the writing of social and economic history was quickly appreciated. In 1926 Mikhail Rostovtzeff published his monumental *Social and Economic History of the Roman Empire*, the first work to acknowledge the life of the common people as a significant component of the study of ancient history. In the preface, Rostovtzeff lamented the fact that he was unable to procure illustrations of objects of daily life, ". . . products of industrial activity, such as pots, lamps, glassware, remains of textiles, jewels, metal work and so forth," for he regarded such illustrations "as an essential part of the book, as essential, in fact, as the notes and the quotations from literary or documentary sources."[12] Three years later as a result of the Karanis excavations, the situation had changed. In 1928, when a German translation of Rostovtzeff's pioneering work was being prepared, the author requested permission to publish plans of the Karanis houses and photographs of some of the objects found in them. In the new edition, Rostovtzeff wrote, "thanks to this complete investigation . . . the everyday life of one of the characteristic villages of the Fayoum is now illustrated in all its details."[13]

Excavations continued at Karanis for eleven seasons. Among the papyri found were documents that illuminate a wide variety of the financial, legal, political and social transactions of the residents. But in addition, the excavators had recovered tens of thousands of artifacts yielding a complete range of material goods: furniture, foodstuffs, tablewares, religious dedications, tools, toys, hair combs, harnesses, clothing—and more. At last, students of the past could observe the "environment of life" in a Graeco-Roman town.

Publishing the Finds

During the course of the excavations and at their close, the Egyptian Department of Antiquities allocated to The University of Michigan an enormous number of objects constituting a representative selection of the finds.[14] These objects, numbering close to 44,000, account for nearly half of the collections presently housed in the Kelsey Museum. The hundreds of papyri found at Karanis are not even included in this tally, for they have been transferred to the Rare Book Collection of the University's Harlan Hatcher Graduate Library. Once the material evidence was in hand, an active program of publication ensued. Even before the field work at Karanis had ended, reports and monographs began to appear. Arthur Boak and Enoch Peterson produced topographical and architectural reports for the seasons of 1924 through 1931 and Lillian Wilson published a selection of textiles in 1933.[15] Soon thereafter, in 1936, Donald Harden's fundamental study of the Roman glass appeared, and articles by numerous scholars followed in rapid succession. Throughout the 1940s and 1950s and into the 1960s studies of papyri and ostraka by Herbert

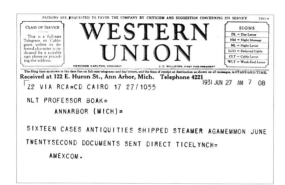

Fig. 9. Telegram from Cairo to Ann Arbor notifying Professor Arthur Book of the arrival of artifacts (Kelsey Museum photograph by Fred Anderegg).

Fig. 10. Hoard of gold coins of the second century AD gathered in a sieve just after they were found (Kelsey Museum Archives, 5.2421).

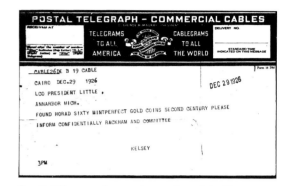

Fig. 11. Telegram informing the president of the University of Michigan of the discovery of the coin hoard (Kelsey Museum photograph by Fred Anderegg).

Youtie, Orsamus Pearl, John Winter and Elinor Husselman and of the coins by Rolfe Haatvedt and Enoch Peterson unleashed a veritable flood of information not only concerning Karanis itself, but the whole of Egypt and its relationship to the Empire of Rome.[16] The University of Michigan moved to the forefront of scholarship in the field of Graeco-Roman Egypt, for which these studies have become standard works of reference.

The care and cataloging of the finds from Karanis, along with the organization of the extensive number of records of the excavation itself, posed a formidable task for those who were in charge of the Museum of Archaeology. Thus, for a number of years the pace of publication slackened. Recently, however, under the inspired leadership of John Griffiths Pedley, current Director of the Kelsey Museum, the cataloging and publication of Karanis

materials has once again become a major focus of energy and activity. Thanks to generous grants from the National Endowment for the Humanities and the National Endowment for the Arts, the objects from Karanis have now been fully entered into the Museum's card catalogue system. In the revitalized Kelsey Museum Studies series three monographs on Karanis have appeared within the past five years: one on lamps by Louise Shier, another on the topography and architecture by Elinor Husselman, and a third, on pottery, by Barbara Johnson; and others are being prepared.[17] The Museum's exhibits program has also fostered publication of bodies of material from Karanis. In 1978, *Guardians*

of the Nile focused attention on the sculptures; in 1980, *The Art of the Ancient Weaver* included selected textiles and weavers' equipment; and in 1982, *Wondrous Glass* featured nearly two hundred whole vessels and fragments from the site.[18] At the same time, a steady stream of publications on Karanis papyri has continued; between 1971 and 1977 several more volumes have appeared.[19] While much more remains to be done, The University of Michigan is moving to fulfill its long-standing obligation to this exceptional site.

The Exhibition

Given this renewed focus on the material from Karanis, the time has come for an exhibition which offers an overview of the excavations and their results. A comprehensive exhibition has not been attempted since 1947 when *Life in Egypt Under Roman Rule* presented papyri and objects from Karanis and two other related sites—Terenouthis and Soknopaiou Nesos—which were explored briefly by the University excavators in Egypt during the 1930s. This exhibition occupied the entire first floor of the Kelsey Museum and documented in great detail all phases of an individual's life from early childhood to the grave.

The present exhibition takes a somewhat different approach to essentially the same theme. Viewed exclusively from the perspective of the town of Karanis, the exhibition centers upon the three aspects of daily life which the Michigan excavations revealed in greatest detail: earning a living, maintaining a home, and worshipping the gods. Limited to less than a quarter of the space used before, this exhibition can pretend neither to do justice to the full potential of these themes that the Karanis collections themselves would allow nor to represent adequately the results that the excavators and various subsequent scholars have attained. Rather, the intention is to evoke for the visitor a vivid impression of the "environment of life" at Karanis and to convey the spirit expressed in the eloquent words of Enoch Peterson, who directed the excavations from 1926 to 1935:

We have seen the letters these people wrote to one another, the accounts they kept in business transactions, the kinds of food they ate, the grain they planted in their irrigated plots of land, the cloth they wove to make their garments, the wooden boxes in which they stored their treasures, the glass that must have been highly cherished, the pottery that served as common household ware, the toys that delighted the hearts of their children, the lamps that gave such feeble light and so much smoke, staining black the niches in their housewalls, and the paintings, all of some religious significance, with which they sometimes adorned their houses. We have seen the very temples in which they worshipped, now in ruins, mute reminders of a cult that even then was in decay. The people who wrote and read the papyri, which have become so valuable as source material for the history of this period, are revealed to us as a living people in a living town.[20]

One may stand in awe of the golden coffins of the pharaonic kings and marvel at the achievements of the master builders and craftsmen of the royal courts, but to ponder the things that reveal the concerns of the common man of ancient times is to touch the thread of continuity that links antiquity to life in our own day.

[1] Hunt, 121–28.
[2] Grenfell, Hunt and Hogarth, 21.
[3] Ibid.
[4] Turner, 161–62.
[5] Ibid., 163.
[6] Grenfell, Hunt and Hogarth, 24.
[7] Petrie, 1892, 3.
[8] Ibid., 164.
[9] Drower, 33.
[10] Kelsey, 17.
[11] Ibid., 26.
[12] Rostovtzeff, 1926, xiv.
[13] Rostovtzeff, second ed., 1931, pp. 289–91, pls. LIV and LV.
[14] Butler, 6–7, reports on the Karanis accessions through 1929.
[15] Boak and Peterson; Boak, 1933; Wilson.
[16] Yeivin; Harden; Boak, 1944-45 and 1947; Husselman, 1952, 1953 and 1958, Youtie and Pearl, 1939 and 1944; Youtie and Winter; Haatvedt and Peterson, among others. See also Geremek, whose study of Karanis depends significantly upon the work of Michigan scholars.
[17] Shier, 1978; Husselman, 1979; Johnson, 1981.
[18] Gazda et al.; Root.
[19] Including Husselman, 1971; Riad and Shelton; and Shelton.
[20] "Unearthing the Past," 9.

THE RURAL ECONOMY

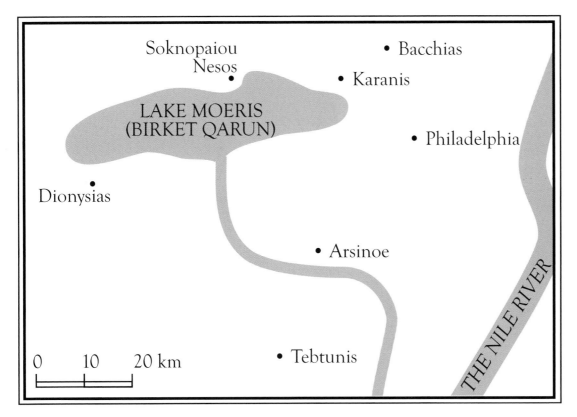

Fig. 12. The Fayum in the Roman period.

Fig. 13. The Fayum basin continues to be Egypt's largest and most fertile area (Kelsey Museum Archives, 209).

Karanis was one of a number of towns established in the Arsinoite nome under Ptolemy II Philadelphus (285–247 BC) as part of a scheme to settle Greek mercenaries among the indigenous Egyptians and to exploit the potential of the fertile Fayum basin. At Karanis periods of prosperity alternated with periods of recession depending in part upon the degree to which the prevailing government maintained the irrigation system that was vital to the productivity of the land. The agricultural richness of the area had long been recognized by Egyptian kings. As early as Dynasty XII (1985– 1773 BC) an elaborate system of locks and canals was constructed under the pharaoh Amenemhat III. Lake Moeris, fed by a branch of the Nile, had once filled much of the oasis area; but by Ptolemaic times its level had been lowered so that much land, especially around the northern shore where Karanis is located, could be reclaimed. The early canals of Amenemhat III had long since fallen into decay when, under the early Ptolemies, a new and extensive irrigation system was put into working order.[1] By the late Ptolemaic period, however, the canals had silted up and embankments caved in, and the agricultural efficiency of the Fayum once again declined.

In 31 BC, Octavian (Augustus) conquered the forces of Antony and Cleopatra at Actium, and in the following year Egypt was added to the growing Roman Empire. Augustus, recognizing the rich resources of his newly conquered territory, moved to restore productivity by sending in the Roman army to clean the canals and rebuild the dikes.[2] The renewed prosperity engendered is marked at Karanis by an expansion of the original Ptolemaic settlement towards the north.[3]

The people of Karanis lived within a world of self-sufficiency, concerned largely with providing for their own basic needs. Yet as subjects of the Roman Emperor, they were obliged to participate in the pattern of services that supported the economy of Rome. This participation took the form of compulsory sharing with the state. A tax in kind was levied upon everything grown by the residents in their fields, while a tax in money was assessed upon most occupations and business transactions. Tax rolls surviving from AD 171–175 list in great detail the individual taxpayers and their payments, arranged according to the types of assessments levied.[4] These documents along with private letters, legal contracts, receipts and census lists, when viewed against the setting in which the people worked and the tools they used to accomplish their tasks, provide a vivid picture of life in a subsistence economy. The peace and political stability brought by Augustus and kept alive by his successors meant prosperity for generations of landholders at Karanis well into the second century AD. In the late second century, and again in the second quarter of the third, there were notable recessions that mirrored difficulties experienced by the Empire at large; but not until the fourth century did the town experience an irreversible decline.

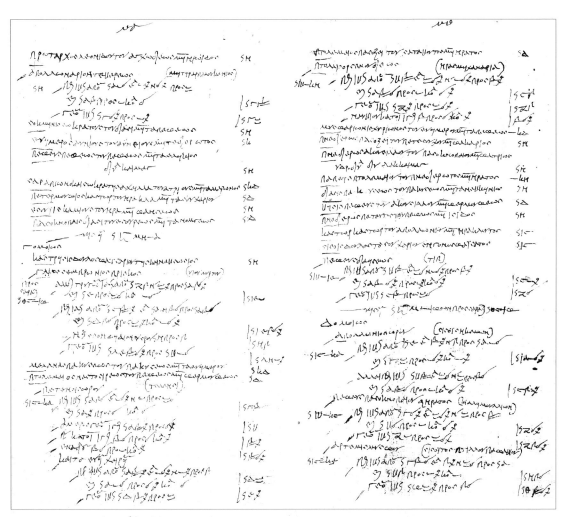

Fig. 14. Tax roll of AD 172–173: A portion of a lengthy papyrus listing names, assessments and amounts (P.Mich. inv. 4171 [= P.Mich. IV 224]). Reproduced with the permission of the Papyrology Collection, Graduate Library, The University of Michigan.

Agriculture

The dietary needs of the people of Karanis were supplied by crops raised on local farms and in gardens. Actual remains of foodstuffs found during the excavations include wheat, barley, lentils, olives, radishes, dates, figs, peaches, pistachios and walnuts.[5] Of these crops durum wheat was by far the most important, both for the town's own subsistence and for the payment of the tithe due to the Roman state.

During the Roman period, farmland in Egypt was owned by temples, private individuals and the state. Temple land was taxed at a fixed rate while private farmers and farmers who had leased state lands were required to pay a portion of their produce to the government. In the case of the state farmer, a rental fee was levied in addition.[6] Private farmers, who often subleased their land, were free to make any sort of agreement they wished with their lessees as to the division of tax payments, supplies of seed and tools and cultivation work. A private letter from the end of the first century AD alludes to one such arrangement:

Apollonous to Terentianus, her brother, greeting, and before all else, good health. I want you to know that since I wrote to you before about my affairs . . . I have reduced your brother's rent to the extent of two artabae. Now I receive from him eight artabae of wheat and six artabae of vegetable seed.[7]

By contrast, the state farmer was closely monitored by the government. He was required to take an oath that he would sow and cultivate specific crops and repay the seed at harvest time into the state granary, and he had to obtain a receipt for each aspect of cultivation which depended upon state supplies, beginning in November with the advance of seed-corn:

Fig. 15. Threshing grain. In the Fayum at the time of the Karanis excavations, farmers processed grain employing methods similar to those used in antiquity (Kelsey Museum Archives, 806).

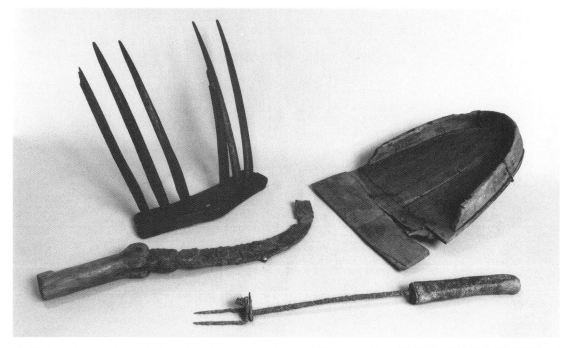

Fig. 16. Agricultural implements include winnowing shovels, cultivators, sickles and pitchforks (KM 3420, KM 3740, KM 3355 and KM 3738; Kelsey Museum photograph by Sue Webb).

To the grain collectors of Karanis: I, Kanis, son of Acchophis, have received an advance of seed-corn, hereby acknowledged, of the twenty-second year of Antoninus Caesar, the lord, the 7 arouras of royal land of Patsontis, belonging to the third cleruchy.[8]

After receiving an allotment of seed, each farmer was responsible for planting and harvesting his own crop. Soil preparation and sowing took place from November through January. Plows, sickles, pitchforks and winnowing shovels, found randomly scattered in houses throughout the town,[9] bear witness to the various farming activities which had formed the backbone of daily life in Egypt for millennia. Even the forms of the farmer's tools had not changed appreciably since Dynastic times.

The harvesting of wheat began during the month of April, and so did the collection of taxes.[10] Harvested grain was brought to the threshing floor where it was recorded and collected. Monthly tallies, as well as many individual receipts recording multiple payments, indicate that the Karanis taxpayer was allowed to pay what was due in installments.[11] From the threshing floor the grain was loaded in sacks and transported to a storage facility. That grain which comprised an individual's payment to the government was taken to one of the many large granaries in the town and exchanged for a receipt from the *sitologus*, or superintendent. As the following example illustrates, such receipts were formal documents acknowledging that the farmer had discharged his duties toward the state:

The sixteenth year of Lucius Septimius Severus Pius Pertinax and Marcus Aurelius Antoninus Pius, Augusti, . . . We Ptolemaios, son of Ptolemaios and Diskoros, son of Mysthes, and their associates in the allotment of the *sitologia* of the village of Karanis, have received at the granary of the aforesaid village by leveled public measure . . . from the produce of the past 15th year, for catoecic dues of Karanis, from Horion son of Apolinarius, eleven twelfths of an artaba of wheat, equals 11/12 artaba of wheat; on the eleventh likewise from the same through Julius, son of Eudas, one artaba of wheat, equals 1 artaba of wheat.[12]

Ten large granaries and seven smaller ones revealed by the excavators underscore the dominant role that grain production played in the local economy. These buildings housed the tax-grain but were also leased for private use.[13] All of the large granaries at Karanis were constructed along lines similar to Roman military storehouses. Rooms used as offices or living quarters fronted onto the street. Behind them was a central courtyard, three sides of which were lined with storage bins or, more often, chambers with vaulted ceilings that reached a height of about three meters above the floor. The interiors of these chambers were subdivided into four or six bins, each about a meter deep. A small window high in the arch provided ventilation.[14] This arrangement conforms remarkably well to the type prescribed by Columella, in his agricultural treatise of the first century AD:

Fig. 17. Granary C123 during excavation; on the right are many individual bins, in the center some vaulted roofs (Kelsey Museum Archives, 7.2368)

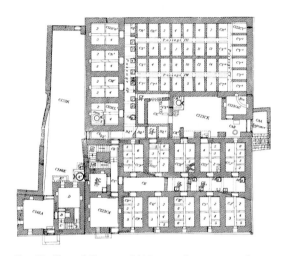

Fig. 18. Plan of Granary C123, one of seventeen such storage facilities excavated at Karanis (Kelsey Museum Archives, M8.694).

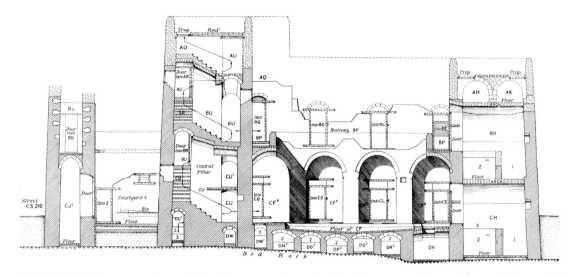

Fig. 19. Vaulted ceilings were used extensively in substructures and main chambers of granaries, as shown in this view of Granary C65 (Kelsey Museum Archives, M8.695).

. . . the best place for storing grain . . . [is] a granary with a vaulted ceiling . . . [and] divided into bins to permit the storage of every kind of legume by itself.[15]

The transport of revenue grain from the village to Alexandria, Egypt's main port during the Graeco-Roman period, was administered by local officials on behalf of the imperial government. Along with the tax-grain itself, farmers paid supplementary amounts as additional tax, all of which were meticulously recorded by the harbor officials:

Aurelios Aphrodisios and Pamiton, receivers of the harbor of Leukogion in the fifth pagus. To Aurelios Kasios and Aurelios Isidoros and their associate sitolo-

goi of the village of Karanis and a part of its horiodeiktia greeting.

We have received from you in the same harbor of Leukogion, including the charges of 10% and 2%, for the canon of the 17th and 5th years of . . . grain on behalf of the village of Karanis and its horiodeiktia clean barley to the amount of exactly one thousand nine hundred seventy-six artabas, 1,976 artabas, and I have also received one denarius on each modius.

In the consulship of our lords Valerius Licinnianus Licinius Augustus and Flavius Valerius Constantinus, son of the Augusti, on the fifth day before the Kalends of September.

(2nd hand) We, Aurelios Aphrodisios and Aurelios Pamiton, receivers, have the one thousand nine hundred sev-

enty-six artabas of barley as aforesaid. I, Aurelios Ap . . . wrote for them since they are illiterate.[16]

At Alexandria the grain was again stored in granaries to await shipment to Rome. The transport of grain provided a wide range of employment for Alexandrians who organized guilds specifically for these journeys. Their ships, sailing in the spring, made the hazardous journey to Italy, some 1,700 miles, in one or two months.[17] The excitement sparked by the imminent arrival of the fleet at Puteoli on the Bay of Naples was recorded in the mid-first century AD by Seneca in a letter to a friend:

Fig. 20. *Olive press base found in the courtyard of House C86 shows grooves which conducted the oil into a large pot (Kelsey Museum Archives, 5.4219).*

Fig. 21. *Group of amphoras. Jars of this type were used to store and transport liquids such as oil and wine (Kelsey Museum Archives, 5.1843).*

Suddenly there came into our view to-day the "Alexandrian" ships,—I mean those which are usually sent ahead to announce the coming of the fleet; . . . The Campanians are glad to see them; all the rabble of Puteoli stand on the docks. . . . everybody was bustling about and hurrying to the waterfront. . . .[18]

By the third quarter of the first century AD grain from Egypt provided food for the city of Rome for four months of the year, making it, along with Africa, the most important source in the early Empire.[19]

Other agricultural products were also abundant in the Fayum. Large tracts of garden land had been preserved by the Ptolemies for the growing of olive trees, vineyards and date palms. As with the grain land, some of these garden lands were owned privately and some by the state. The maintenance of this property was expensive, since it generally occupied higher ground which was troublesome to irrigate. In periods of economic decline the greater part of these holdings fell out of use;[20] but during times of prosperity, the investment in their upkeep was compensated for by rich returns. Strabo, describing the geography of the region in which Karanis was located, made these remarks on its productivity:

This nome is the most noteworthy of all in respect to its appearance, its fertility, and its material development, for it alone is planted with olive trees that are large and full-grown and bear fine fruit, . . . and it produces wine in no small quantity, as well as grain, pulse, and the other seed-plants in very great varieties.[21]

The tax records show that almost half the population of Karanis paid rental on garden lands. Within the houses were found many objects and installations connected with the cultivation of olive groves and vineyards and the processing of their fruits. Large crushing stones and olive presses were found in several courtyards, along with propping sticks for grape vines, and a cultivator's knife. The knife, of Greek rather than native Egyptian design, was used to cut the grape clusters from the vine, thus avoiding damage caused by hand picking.[22]

In spite of all the local production evidenced by the material remains, the people of Karanis occasionally supplemented their provisions with imported goods. Large numbers of amphoras, used to store and ship wine and oil, were recovered at the site. Many of these containers had been imported from Africa, and one had come from Brindisi in Italy. Their contents, more costly than the local product, were presumably of a higher quality. A comment by Strabo might explain why imports were desirable even when local produce was at hand:

[The] olive trees . . . would also produce good olive oil if the olives were carefully gathered. But since they [i.e. the residents] neglect this matter, although they make much oil, it has a bad smell. . . .[23]

Another important aspect of the rural economy was the raising of pigeons. Portions of six dovecotes were found at Karanis, but it is likely that there were many more. Since dovecotes were commonly built in the upper story of a house or tower, they would have been the first part of a structure to collapse. Often, they were built directly above or adjacent to a granary. Their walls of sun-dried brick were lined

Fig. 22. Dovecote C65. This inside view shows the orderly arrangement of pots, each of which served as a nest (Kelsey Museum Archives, 5.3489).

been necessary. In fact, two of the excavated dovecotes contained space for at least 250 birds, suggesting that they were commercial establishments. The tax rolls show that dovecote assessments were collected at Karanis from twelve people in the period from AD 173 to 175. Throughout the Fayum, this tax was levied annually as a licensing fee.[27]

In addition to pigeons, a number of different animals were raised for food, transport, and work on the land. The faunal remains recovered during the excavations include horses, mules, cows, sheep, pigs, dogs and gazelles, and the tax rolls add camels and donkeys to this group. Assessments were levied in particular on camels, donkeys and pigs, whose owners were organized in guilds which produced annual lists of individual members and their holdings. One such declaration was made by a camel-keeper in AD 134:

I, Dioskoros, . . . from the village of Karanis, camelherd of the same village, swear by the Fortune of Emperor Caesar Trajan Hadrian Augustus that I declare fifty-five full-grown camels in the village, that is 55, and 16 colts, making altogether 72 camels.[28]

These lists were made in part to provide accurate information for taxation and in part because owners were required to lend certain animals (e.g., camels and donkeys) to the state, either for the transport of grain or for work on canal embankments.[29]

Another levy assessed by the state was a meat tax, payed to a special official and used to feed troops stationed in the area. Since farmers generally had little hard currency, the tax was often paid in kind. A receipt from AD 313 shows that large quantities of meat were collected:

with horizontally placed pots—each pot serving as the nesting place for one bird.[24] Many of these pots were found still in place, but others were scattered throughout the site.[25] The advantages of raising pigeons were enumerated by Columella:

. . . the keeping of animals at the farm . . . brings no small profit to farmers, since they use the dung of fowls to doc-tor . . . every kind of soil, and with the fowls themselves they enrich the family kitchen and table by providing rich fare; and, lastly, with the price which they obtain by selling . . . they increase the revenue of the farm.[26]

A private farmer working on a small scale could obtain enough manure and food for his own needs, but to turn a profit a larger operation would have

Fig. 23. Terracotta figurines depict some of the animals common in the rural environment of Karanis (KM 6892, KM 6886, KM 6878, KM 3751 and KM 6879; Kelsey Museum photograph by Sue Webb).

The Aurelioi, Dioskoros and Son of Di . . . , and Ptolemaios, son of Herakleos, and Eudaimon, son of Doulos, collectors of meat for the village of Karanis and its district, to Isidoros, son of Ptolemaios, greeting.

We have received from you for meat of the eighth, sixth and fourth year, thirty and one-half pounds of pork, and on behalf of . . . son of Palemon, thirteen pounds, and . . . nineteen pounds, making in all sixty-two and one-half pounds.

In the second consulship of our Lords Constantine and Licinius, Phaophi 23.[30]

In addition to the faunal remains and the written documents, equipment such as ox halters, donkey and camel saddles, muzzles and tethering stakes found in and around many homes indicate the constant presence of animals in the environment. Many terracotta figurines of camels, cows, boars, birds, horses and dogs vividly reinforce our impression of the importance of these animals in daily life

at Karanis. Some of these figurines may have been children's toys, but others must surely have had votive significance.

Crafts

The textile industry was second only to agriculture as the most extensively taxed in Roman Egypt. It was also a highly specialized occupation, with at least eighteen categories of employment.[31] Four of these specialties appear in the Karanis tax rolls— wool shearers, weavers, fullers and wool sellers. At Karanis the sheep shearers were taxed as a guild associated with the temple. The shearers and sellers themselves apparently did not engage in the raising of sheep, as the tax receipts document payment by other persons for the rental of pastureland.[32]

An extraordinary number of textiles, approximately 3,500 pieces, were recovered in the excavations. Of these, more than ninety percent were either wool or linen, and wool was by far the more prevalent.[33] Both the availability of wool at Karanis and the many spinning and weaving tools found in the excavations make it likely that much weaving was done in the town. The mention in the tax rolls of a weaver, and a fuller to dye the threads or cloth, implies the same.

Most households undoubtedly engaged in the combing, spinning and weaving of cloth for their own use, but at least one aspect of textile manufacture was not purely domestic—the compulsory supply of clothing for the military. This charge was laid upon small towns as well as large cities throughout Egypt and was well established by the early second century AD. A document records that the village

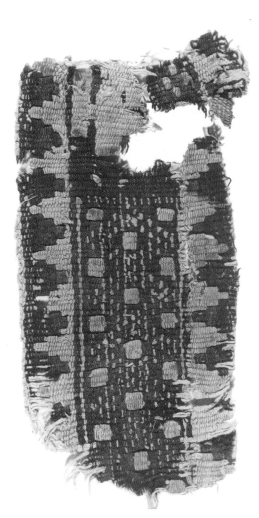

Fig. 24. Textile fragment: At Karanis, the dry climate fostered the preservation of more than 3,500 pieces of cloth (KM 11192; Kelsey Museum photograph by Fred Anderegg).

of Karanis supplied twenty-four tunics and eight cloaks for the years AD 310–311. Because the receipt actually dates from the year AD 314, it has been suggested that it may have taken three years to weave all the garments requisitioned.[34] An earlier receipt, dated to AD 298, records the partial fulfillment of the village's annual quota; the amount involved indicates that in the eyes of a compulsive bureaucrat, no number was too low for a preliminary payment:

Aurelii Sempronius and Agathinus and Siloeis, supervisors of cloaks, to Aurelius Ptollarion, komarch of Karanis, greetings. We have received from you on behalf of the same village one cloak, equals 1 cloak, I, Aurelius Sempronius, wrote the entire receipt.[35]

Pottery vessels of every sort were used by residents of the town. Yet, despite the availability of clay and the relative ease of manufacture, it is difficult to know how much of the pottery found at Karanis was actually made there. That a few people specialized in this craft is, however, clear; the tax rolls of AD 173–175 record the payment of the potter's tax by four persons.[36] Many of the utilitarian wares are made from Nile clay, including two dozen pigeon pots that were discovered not far from a large circular structure thought to be a kiln. This structure, made entirely of burnt brick, lacks the adobe and mud plaster casing common for ovens found in homes. Both the construction, which would allow for a more intense heat, and the larger size suggest commercial use. Such a kiln would have made possible the firing of a wide va-

Fig. 25. Pottery kiln. The thick wall visible on the left indicated a capacity to sustain high temperatures (Kelsey Museum Archives, 5.1662).

riety of terracotta objects, including lamps and small figurines.[37]

Glass vessels were found by the hundreds at Karanis, a great many of them intact. More than half of the complete pieces occurred in groups or hoards. The sheer volume of glass discovered, over twice as much as at any other single site in Egypt, has led to the assumption that glass was manufactured at Karanis. It is possible that a glass factory was located near the town's center, which had been completely destroyed by the sebbakhin prior to excavations. No definitive evidence was recovered, however, to prove that these vessels were made locally. Neither a workshop area nor any glass-making tools were identified, and no glass tax appears in the second-century AD tax rolls. On the other hand, a majority of the glass from Karanis was found in fourth- and fifth-century AD levels,

Fig. 26. Decanter and goblets. Thin walls and uniform shapes reflect the skill attained by Egyptian glass blowers (KM 5936, KM 5950 and KM 5963–KM 5966; Kelsey Museum photograph by Ken Pokorny).

corresponding to that period of mass production in the glass industry which was encouraged by Constantine's remittance of the glass tax.[38]

The greater part of the Karanis glass consists of those common bowls and plates which are not likely to have been imported. However, many finer pieces were recovered which were surely acquired in Alexandria, a city famed for its production of luxury glass in the Roman period. A letter, from a son stationed in Alexandria to his father in Karanis, vividly corroborates this assumption:

Know, father, that I have received the things that you sent me. . . . I thank you because you considered me worthy and have made me free from care. I have sent you, father . . . sets of glassware, two bowls of quinarius size, a dozen goblets. . . .[39]

Trade

Karanis was located advantageously for participation in the larger economic system of the Empire. A gateway into one of Egypt's most densely populated regions, it was both a point of departure for caravans and a station for the desert police.[40] About 125 miles to the north, and easily accessible by water, lay Alexandria, one of the great emporia of the Roman Empire. Through her port passed every conceivable luxury item from abroad, and the city itself produced an assortment of material goods matched only by Rome. Dio Chrysostom, writing in the first century AD, describes Alexandria as follows:

. . . ranked second among all cities beneath the sun. . . . The trade, not merely of islands, ports, a few straits and isthmuses, but of practically the whole world is yours. For Alexandria is situated, as it were, at the crossroads of the whole world, of even the most remote nations thereof, as if it were a market serving a single city, a market which brings together into one place all manner of men, displaying them to one another, and, as far as possible, making them a kindred people.[41]

Many of the luxury objects found at Karanis, such as jewelry, sculpture, ivory combs and inlaid boxes, were undoubtedly purchased in Alexandria. Such goods were, however, available elsewhere in the Empire, as a letter from a soldier stationed in Syria to his mother in Karanis implies:

I received some money and wanted to send you a gift of Tyrian wares; and since you did not reply, I have not entrusted it to anyone on account of the length of the

Fig. 27. Bronze objects as found in a large storage jar included an incense stand (right) and a pitcher (center) (Kelsey Museum Archives, 5.2719).

Fig. 28. Platter and bowls of fine red slip ware imported from the Roman provinces of Africa (KM 7160, KM 7142 and KM 7156; Kelsey Museum photograph by Sue Webb).

journey. For fine garments and ebony and pearls and unguents are brought here in abundance. Therefore I ask you, my lady, to be . . . and merrily joyful; for this is a good place.[42]

In addition to the types of luxury items mentioned, much of the ceramic tableware was also imported. It is of the type known as African Red Slip, which was produced in North African factories from the mid-third century until the fifth century AD.[43] This pottery, which was the daily tableware throughout much of the Empire, constituted the finer tableware of the typical Karanis household.

For most of the town's residents, dependence on the land and assessments by the state precluded the amassing of great wealth which would have allowed for a luxurious mode of life. While the finds are partly composed of the finer products of larger centers, most of the artifacts, including many of the imported ones, reflect the simple manner in which life was lived in a Roman farming community.

[1] Diodorus I, 61; Kees, 1961, 220-23 and 227-28; Geremek, 41-52.

[2] Wallace, 2.

[3] Peterson in Boak, 1933, 54.

[4] Youtie and Pearl, 1939, viii and ix.

[5] Leighty and Bartlett in Boak, 1933.

[6] Wallace, 1-3; Geremek, 53-70.

[7] Youtie and Winter, 5 (P.Mich. inv. 6001)

[8] Husselman, 1971, 60, Goodspeed, 8 (#1, text, p. 18).

[9] Bellah, 4-5.

[10] Packman, 59; Youtie and Pearl, 1944, 41.

[11] The Karanis tax rolls list the following subsidiary charges (Youtie and Pearl, 1944, 24):
dichoinikia: a crown tax of 1/20th of an artaba per aroura of land, retained from the Ptolemaic period (Johnson, 1936, 508);
prosmetroumena: a supplementary charge, originally imposed by Augustus as compensation for differences in the content of local measures used in collecting grain dues and those specified by the state for accepting tax payments (Boak, 1947, 27; Wallace, 38);
pentarabia: a 5% tax when payment was made in barley rather than wheat (Johnson, 1936, 511);
dragmategia: a charge for transporting sheaves from the field to the threshing floor (Johnson, 1936, 508).
The installment system was originally developed under the early Ptolemies and was adopted by the Romans. Packman, 55; Youtie and Pearl, 1944, 23-25, 41.

[12] Youtie and Pearl, 1944, 100 (P.Mich. inv. 2923).

[13] Husselman, 1952, 58, 70.

[14] Rickman, 1971, 263; Husselman, 1952, 59-60, 63.

[15] Columella, I.6.12-13.

[16] Boak, 1947, 30 (Cairo, Journal d'entrée no. 57394).

[17] Wallace, 45-46; Rickman, 1980, 14.

[18] Seneca, Ep., 77.

[19] Josephus, Bell Iud., 2.386; Rickman, 1980, 231.

[20] Kees, 1961, 228-29.

[21] Strabo, 17.1.35.

[22] Bellah, 6.

[23] Strabo, 17.1.35.

[24] Columella, VIII.8.1; Varro, III.7.1.

[25] Husselman, 1953, 83, n. 4.

[26] Columella, VIII.1.2.

[27] Husselman, 1953, 84, 86, 90; Youtie and Pearl, 1939, 136-37; Wallace, 69.

[28] Husselman, 1971, 55-57 (P.Mich. inv. 5895). The error in addition (15 + 56 = 71, not 72) seems to have been the fault of the scribe.

[29] Wallace, 92.

[30] Boak, 1944-45, 20.

[31] Papyri and ostraka which record the receipts of taxes show the following subdivisions of the weaver's trade (Wallace, 193-202; Johnson, 1936, 538-44): weaver, dyer, weaver of fine linen, web beater, fuller, wool dealer, wool shearer, wool seller, wool/web beater, weaver of striped patterns, master of looms, weaver of heavy garments, vendor of fleece, flax spinner, flax seller, linen weaver, washer and treater of cloth and weaver of tapestries.

[32] Youtie and Pearl, 1939, 140; Shelton, 100.

[33] Wilson, 9. 2,800 pieces were identified as wool, 350 as linen.

[34] Jones, 186-87; Boak, 1947, 30-33.

[35] Husselman, 1971, 65 (P.Mich. inv. 5065a).

[36] Youtie and Pearl, 1944, vol. II, 140; Shelton, 100.

[37] Peterson, vol. II, 835-36; Shier, 1978, 5; Allen in Gazda et al., 58-61; Johnson, 1981, 1-3.

[38] Harden, 34-38, 40; Codex Theod., 13.4.2.

[39] Youtie and Winter, 32 (P.Mich. inv. 5390).

[40] Kees, 1961, 228.

[41] Dio Chrysostom, 32.36.40.

[42] Youtie and Winter, 9 (P.Mich. inv. 5888).

[43] Johnson, 1981, 9-10; Hayes, 108.

DOMESTIC LIFE

In unearthing hundreds of dwellings at Karanis the excavators took care to preserve the integrity of each house and its contents. Many of the furnishings, however, had already been removed by the occupants themselves when they abandoned the town. Yet those which were left behind, when viewed in conjunction with official documents and personal letters of the homeowners, provide a vivid impression of the domestic concerns of the average household at Karanis in Roman times.

The Houses

The multi-storied houses of Karanis were sturdy and unpretentious, built to suit the needs of rural families who labored to provide for themselves the basic necessities of life. They were grouped in blocks, or *insulae*, which often grew by a process of accretion, with the result that many streets tended to meander.[1] Although there were two broad main roads running north and south through the town, the other streets, which were narrow, would frequently come to a dead end or be obstructed by building extensions. Within each block, houses shared party walls and occasionally a courtyard, but otherwise they were independent, self-sufficient structures.[2] Throughout the entire history of the town, these houses were of a consistently functional design. Underground rooms were used for storage while an open-air courtyard on the ground floor was the focus of much of the domestic activity. Other rooms, on the ground level and on upper stories, were arranged around a continuous stairway which connected all of the floors.[3]

The multi-storied construction was sometimes necessitated by the rapid accumulation of sand blown in from the desert during wind storms and of debris from the routines of daily life. When this occurred, the level of the streets would rise and the lower stories

Fig. 29. Partial street plan of late layer C dating from the second to the mid third century AD (Kelsey Museum Archives, M8.1044).

Fig. 30. Interior view of houses near the North Temple; the house at left preserves a line of beam holes (Kelsey Museum Archives, 5.1928).

"KARANIS"
(KOM-AUSHIM)

SECTIONS : F10 & G10

From North to South Looking East

KEY

 Brick Walls

 Stone Walls

 Dressed Masonry

 Brick Arches

Wooden Beams

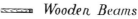 Brick Floor

Mud Floor

Earth

Bed Rock

Field Director *Enoch E. Peterson*

Surveyor *T. Terentieff*

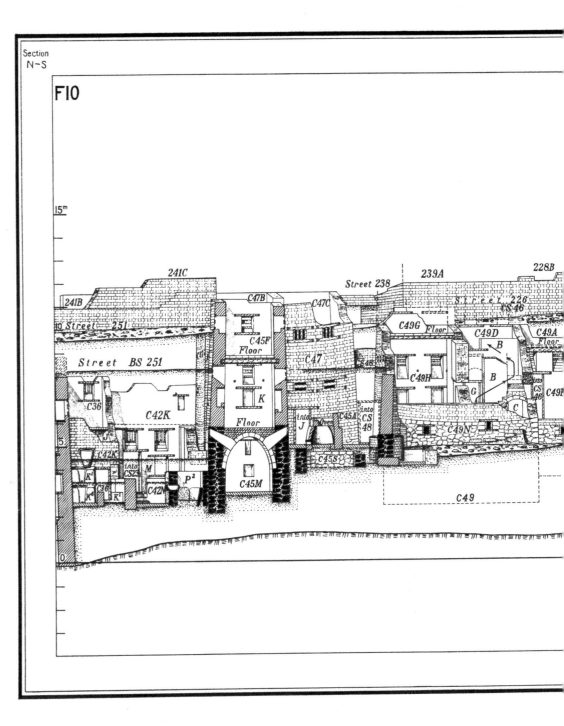

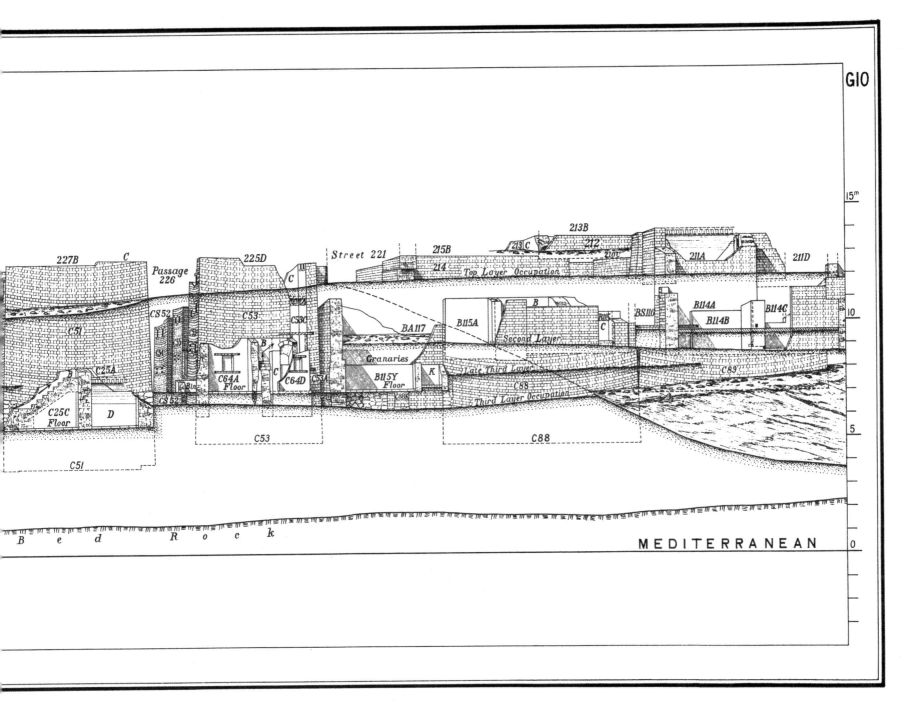

GI0

227B   C

Passage
226

CS 52

225D

Street 221

215B

213B

213 C   212

211

214   Top Layer Occupation

211A

211D

C51

C

C53

C53C

C522

BA 117

B115A

B

Second Layer

B114A

BS 110

B114B

B114C

C

C25A

EI

B

C

C

Granaries

B115Y
Floor

K

Late Third Layer

C88

C89

C25C
Floor

D

CS 52

Bin

C64A
Floor

C64D

C53A

C88

Third Layer Occupation

C51

C53

C88

15ᵐ

10

5

B   e   d   R   o   c   k

MEDITERRANEAN

0

Scale

100   0   1   2   3   4   5   6   7   8   9   10 Metres

Fig. 31. North-South section through the mound of Karanis taken at square F10–G10 (Kelsey Museum Archives, M8.1151).

21

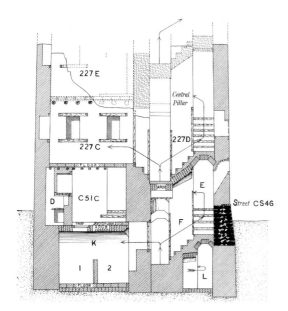

Fig. 32. House C51. Underground rooms were connected to the upper three floors by a continuous staircase, as shown at the right in this drawing (Kelsey Museum Archives, 5.5005).

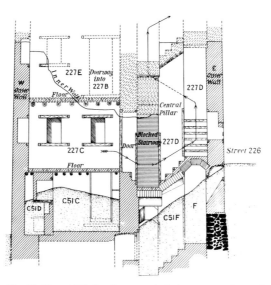

Fig. 33. House C51. In a later period, the basement and ground floor had filled up with sand and the street was at a higher level (Kelsey Museum Archives, 5.5498).

Fig. 34. Walls of mud brick laid in concave beds appear to sag in this view along Street C552 (Kelsey Museum Archives, 828).

Fig. 35. Roof beams of House B109 after removal of a layer of mud bricks; the beams are actually large limbs of trees (Kelsey Museum Archives, 5.2807).

of the houses would be abandoned. Upper floors would be salvaged and a new house constructed on top of the old. Sometimes only the floors of the rooms on the street level would be raised and new windows and doorways constructed at higher levels.[4] Constant alteration of standing structures occurred simultaneously with the building of new ones, so that houses built in different periods stood side by side.

Although the houses were structurally self-contained, the papyri indicate that it was common for a person to own just a fraction of a house.[5] Multiple ownership usually resulted from the fact that children inherited their father's property, but sometimes their fractions of the family property were sold to other individuals. A census declaration from Karanis, dating from AD 189, shows that these arrangements could become exceedingly complicated:

There belong to the persons whose interest I represent, to Tasoucharion, whose father is unknown, her mother being Sarapias, an Antinoite, the mother of the persons named below, a house and courtyard and a third share of another house in the village, and to Gaia Apolinaria and Gemellus

Horion, her children, Antinoites, in common and equally, a house and two courtyards formerly the property of Valeria Diodora and a third share of two houses and two courtyards, and elsewhere a half share of a house and courtyard and of another courtyard, and elsewhere a house and courtyard, and two courtyards formerly the property of Gaius Longinus Apolinarius, veteran, and a house and courtyard formerly the property of Ptolemais, and elsewhere a third share of a house and courtyard, which I declare for the house by house registration of the past 28th year. . . .[6]

The need for adequate space to accommodate entire families must have led to a judicious regard for the cost of building materials and common sense in putting those materials to use. Apart from instances of practical necessity, stone was rarely used. Although easy to find in the outcroppings to the north and east of the town, the expense of hauling it overland may well have proved prohibitive. It was used with some regularity only for the exterior stairs, leading from the street to the doorway or from the house into the courtyard, and occasionally it was also employed in foundations and underground rooms. Sometimes it was inserted along the lower portions of exterior walls that faced the street to prevent them from being damaged by passing traffic.[7] The walls themselves, however, were built of economical mud-brick, which would have been manufactured nearby.[8] In order to prevent the walls of the house from cracking, most builders in Karanis employed a novel technique of bricklaying. On the interior of the house, bricks were set in horizontal courses, but on the exterior they were bedded in a concave foundation. This method caused the outer walls to appear to sag, but cracks did not develop

Fig. 36. Room of House C51, showing simply constructed windows set high into the wall above the niches (Kelsey Museum Archives, 5.2756).

because none of the horizontal and vertical seams continued through the thickness of the walls.[9]

The wide extent of irrigation allowed for the planting of trees such as sycamore, palm and acacia, which, in addition to providing welcome shade, were also used for house construction. In many houses

roughly shaped tree trunks were inserted at various intervals between the course of brick so that irregular projections of the sawn-off branches would prevent the bricks from shifting position. Flat roofs, ceilings and floors were generally built of closely spaced rafters made of large limbs of trees.[10] (Underground rooms of the house, however, were usually vaulted or domed.) Wood was also used extensively for windows, doorways, cupboards and as corner reinforcements on the exteriors of buildings instead of stone. The framework for a window was very simple. Wooden planks were set into the wall on all four sides of a rectangular opening, and horizontal or vertical planks were placed across. Apparently the only function of these windows was to admit light and air, for they were too small and too high on the walls (just below the ceilings) to provide a view. Because their high position also ensured privacy, there was little necessity for devices to close them. In all of Karanis only two windows were found with shutters attached. Sometimes, however, the openings between the bars were blocked with rolled up fabric or baskets.[11]

By contrast to the often crudely constructed windows, doorframes were usually fitted with well-tooled joints, and high standards of craftsmanship were lavished upon the doors themselves. One well-preserved door has recessed panels framed by precisely cut moldings. Interestingly, the side that faced the street is more carefully worked. As all doors in the houses of Karanis, this one turned on pivots that fit into sockets in the threshold and lintel of the frame.[12] Outer doors were provided with sliding wooden bolts or locks, a variety of which were found.

Fig. 37. Two doors, both finely made, as found in House B198; the door in front is now in the Kelsey Museum (KM 24892; Kelsey Museum Archives, 5.3483).

Fig. 38. Bolt case, key and staple. By inserting the key into the upper slot in the bolt case and lifting the three tumblers, the bolt in the lower slot could slide out of its locked position. The staple was fastened to the door jamb to hold the bolt when the door was locked. Bolt and outer two tumblers are restorations (KM 7432, KM 10227 and KM 10238; Kelsey Museum photograph by Sue Webb).

The Furnishings

Heavy, bolted doors along with high, barred windows provided a considerable degree of security for the homeowners, their families and their possessions. Indeed, it seems that many people took a certain pride in the decoration and furnishing of the interiors of their homes. Frequently, interior walls were plastered and covered with a dark wash over which white lines were painted along the horizontal seams between the courses of brick.[13] On these walls no doubt there were cloth hangings; and in wealthier residences, frescoes of religious subjects were also found. The furnishings that were found attest that a considerable measure of comfort and convenience was sought. Mats, and possibly cushions, covered parts of the floor and there were wooden stools, tables, beds, storage boxes and chests, each of a functional, and often aesthetically pleasing, design.

Traditionally in Egypt, stools rather than chairs were the most common form of seat.[14] In fact, in Dynastic times chairs were regarded as symbols of status and honor and would not have been part of the average domestic assemblage.[15] The only chair found at Karanis was one in miniature—a child's toy; but it may give an idea of the type of chair that would have graced homes of the well-to-do. Stools, on the other hand, were found in abundance. Usually their round seats were supported by three legs which, in the finer examples, had been turned on a lathe. The three-legged design, common in antiquity, was the most practical for use on the uneven surfaces of a mud-brick or mat-covered floor, since

Fig. 39. Small tripod table acquired by purchase in the Fayum; numerous fragments of this type of table were found at Karanis. The three-legged design provided stability on uneven mud-brick floors (KM 10220; Kelsey Museum photograph by Fred Anderegg).

the balance could be more easily adjusted on three legs than on four.[16] Most of the tables found during the excavations are also of this sturdy design. These round topped, three-legged tables and stools reflect the influence of Greek and Roman traditions of

Fig. 40. Inlaid reading stand acquired by purchase in the Fayum. Less elaborate but similar examples were found at Karanis; the curved top was designed to support open papyrus scrolls (KM 24808; Kelsey Museum photograph by Fred Anderegg).

Fig. 41. Terracotta and glass lamps; the cord on the lantern is a restoration (KM 7716, KM 5544 and KM 3633; Kelsey Museum photograph by Sue Webb).

ant craftsmen who traveled with the tools of their trade. That furniture was imported at least on occasion is proven by a letter from a young soldier to his father in Karanis. Among the many things he writes of sending is a wooden bed of which, however, only the frame was to reach its destination. The letter reads, in part:

I have sent you, father, by Martialis a bag sewn together, in which you have two mantles, two capes, two linen towels, two sacks, and a wooden bed. I had bought the last together with a mattress and a pillow, and while I was lying ill on the ship they were stolen from me. . . .[20]

The number of wooden reading stands found in the excavations indicates that literacy, while by no means universal, had been attained by more than a few. In fact the same letter in which the army boy announces that he is shipping clothing and a bed to his father also lists "two papyrus rolls for school use, ink inside the papyrus, [and] five pens" among the items being sent. Clearly, supplies for teaching children to read and write were in demand.[21] The majority of stands are simply ornamented with incised grooves.

In the dark rooms of the houses light was provided for reading by various kinds of lamps. Conical glass lamps were probably set into tripod holders or suspended on ropes or chains.[22] These lamps, many of which were found at Karanis, would have been filled entirely with oil or with water covered by a thin layer of oil. When ignited the oil would have given a muted but adequate light. A less fragile and, perhaps therefore, more common type of oil lamp was made of terracotta.[23] A handle was provided

on one end and a wick made of plant fibers or rolled up cloth projected from a hole at the other. These lamps were designed to sit on a flat surface and could easily be moved about. Often they were placed in terracotta lanterns which hung on ropes, probably from pegs in the walls. The opening in the lantern directed the light from the small lamp while simultaneously acting as a shade. In a number of homes small wall niches, blackened by smoke, evidently had also served as lamp holders.[24]

There were no closets in the houses of Karanis, but storage was provided in other ways. Household goods such as pottery and glass tableware were placed in niches recessed in the wall, just below the window, or set into spaces below the stairway.[25] Often the niches were furnished with shelves and occasionally with mud-plaster moldings along the edge of the sill to prevent objects from rolling out.[26]

furniture making rather than that of the ancient Egyptians, which favored tables of rectangular form.[17] Also, in contrast to lightweight, portable Egyptian tables, the tables found at Karanis are rather large and heavy, following the Roman preference for substantial pieces that served as relatively stationary stands.[18] Lathe-turned legs are another sign of Graeco-Roman influence, for the lathe was a Greek invention of the seventh century BC.[19]

How much of the furniture found at Karanis was actually made there is hard to say. No elaborate tools, like lathes, were discovered but it is possible that such equipment would not have been abandoned. On the other hand, finely worked furniture may have been imported or made by itiner-

An assemblage of objects found on a window ledge in a house of the second century AD gives some idea of what the contents of a typical cupboard might have been. Along with a pottery bowl, there were six pieces of glass, two baskets, several weaving implements, a terracotta lamp, a stirring stick, and two combs.[27]

Chests and boxes in a wide assortment of shapes, sizes and materials provided another means of storing goods. These were often made of variously woven reeds and rushes, but wood was also common, and for small containers bone, and even ebony, was used. The simplest boxes resembled crates. One, which contained a number of pieces of the red slip tableware imported from Roman Africa, may have been the same box in which the pottery had been shipped. Nicely crafted and decorated chests must have been intended for the most treasured of possessions, such as imported cut glass, thin-walled pottery, or items of finely woven cloth, while diminutive versions, some of which were fitted with hinged lids, latches and locks, would have held jewelry and other small valuables.[28] Often the interiors of the large as well as small containers were intricately subdivided for organizing the items to be stored.[29] Little baskets and boxes with no provision for securing the lids probably held more ordinary items such as toilette and cosmetic articles—hairpins, combs, kohl jars and kohl sticks.[30] The use of kohl, a type of black eye paint, had been common in Egypt since Predynastic times. Originally its purpose was to ward off insects and infection,[31] and it was worn by men as well as women. The sticks with which

Fig. 42. Cupboard niche in the wall of House C57; within the niche a wooden shelf is well preserved (Kelsey Museum Archives. 5.2800).

Fig. 43. Assemblage of objects found on the window ledge of House BC61 (KM 3787–8, KM 5553, KM 5563, KM 3634, KM 5532–3, KM 5524, KM 5511, KM 3441, KM 3567, KM 10117, KM 3903 a–b, KM 3708, KM 3860, KM 3658, KM 3669 and Cairo 51415; Kelsey Museum Archives, 5.2358).

it was applied were often delicately ornamented. The same was true of hairpins, a number of which found at Karanis were carved at one end with a hand holding a ball.[32] Combs, too, were often intricately incised with geometric or figural designs.[33]

Daily Activities

At Karanis many of the traditional crafts such as basketry, weaving and carpentry were plied in the home. The scene of much of this activity was the courtyard of the house. Mats and baskets, which were found in virtually every dwelling, were woven to fulfill a variety of needs.[34] Items of basketry, for example, were not only used for storing household accessories but also as containers for dry foods and as sieves for sifting granular materials and straining beer. Other

practical objects, such as pot stands and brooms, were also made of reeds and rushes. The typical broom had a rope rather than a long stick for a handle, probably intended for hanging on a courtyard wall.[35]

Cloth for domestic use was also made at home. The combing of the raw fibers to align them for spinning might well have been relegated to the outdoors, but the spinning of the thread could have been done almost anywhere within the house. The spindles and whorls of all sizes indicate that a variety of thread was produced from coarse to fine. Although no looms were found, some parts of them, such as heddles, along with comb and pin beaters, attest to the weaving that was done in the home. Scissors and needles of various sizes were put to use in making hangings and pillow covers as well as most of the family's garments. Yet despite the ability to weave and sew, the average person's wardrobe

was probably quite small. A letter from the second century AD from a young man stationed in Alexandria to his father in Karanis suggests as much:

I ask and beg you, father, for I have no one dear to me except you, after the gods, to send to me by Valerius . . . a cloak, and a girdled tunic, together with my trousers, so that I may have them, since I wore out my tunic before I entered the service. . . .[36]

Another commonly practiced craft was that of carpentry. Finds of mallets, axes, augurs, drills, plumb bobs and a measuring stick confirm that homeowners were equipped to handle minor remodeling and repairs.[37] It is likely, in fact, that many of the simpler furnishings and pieces of household equipment were made at home. Some tools, however, might have served purposes other than those of the carpenter. Mallets, for example, might have

Fig. 44. Small boxes and personal items—two combs, hair pins, kohl sticks, a bracelet and two rings (KM 3327, KM 7702a–b, KM 7551a–b, KM 7673, KM 9974, KM 3488, KM 21773, KM 21781, KM 21783, KM 21814–15, KM 21835, KM 21776, KM 21790, 21772, KM 21844, KM 21847, KM 21869, KM 24079 and KM 23099–100; Kelsey Museum photograph by Sue Webb).

Fig. 45. Baskets showing some of the forms and techniques that were commonly employed (KM 3361a–b, KM 3369, KM 3382 and KM 3442; Kelsey Museum photograph by Fred Anderegg).

Fig. 46. Tools for making cloth—spindles and whorls (with modern yarn), yarn bowl, comb and pin beaters, crochet hooks and sewing needles (KM 3353a–b, KM 7641a–b, KM 24674, KM 7454, KM 21768–71, KM 21919, KM 21925 and KM 23979; Kelsey Museum photograph by Sue Webb).

Fig. 47. Cooking pots, bowls, rope and other objects as found in the storage bin of the courtyard of House C137 (Kelsey Museum Archives, 5.3475).

Fig. 48. Large pythos (storage jar) of a type commonly used for the storage of grain in the courtyards of houses (Kelsey Museum Archives, 5.2186).

Fig. 49. Oven. The upper portion of the curving terracotta walls has been removed along with the insulating casing (Kelsey Museum Archives, 5.3996).

Fig. 50. Theban mill. Small handmills of an ancient Egyptian design were widely used at Karanis (Kelsey Museum Archives, 5.1571).

Fig. 51. Stacks of olive pressings (formerly identified as unleavened bread) used for fuel or animal fodder, found in Granary A411 (KM 4797; Kelsey Museum Archives, 5.1576)

been used for pounding flax to prepare it for spinning.[38] Drills, too, could have been adapted for purposes other than boring holes into wood. Two drill stocks found at Karanis were designed to hold different types of bits, including wooden pegs for starting fires.[39]

Ovens, grain bins, millstones and mortars, along with cooking pots and jars for the storage of foods, show that the courtyard also served as the kitchen of the house. The baking of bread involved the milling of the coarse grain which was stored in rectangular bins or in large vessels (*pithoi*) sunk into the ground. Several kinds of mortars and grinding stones were used to convert grain into flour, but a traditional Egyptian device known as the Theban mill was also used. The Theban mill was designed so that one person could provide the amount of flour needed by an average household for a single day.[40] Those found at Karanis were attached to bases that stood at a comfortable waist-height.[41] That this piece of equipment was regarded as having some value is shown by a receipt of sale:

. . .Thatres . . . acknowledges to Pnepheros . . . that she has sold him . . . the Theban mill that belongs to her, Thatres, with netherstone and handle, just as it is and not subject to rejection; and that she, Thatres, has received from Pnepheros the price agreed upon, twenty-eight silver drachmas. . . .[42]

Circular clay ovens seem to have been constructed piece by piece within the courtyard itself. As each section was formed in clay it was fired, and then all of the parts were assembled. An opening was left at the top for putting fuel, as well as the bread to

Fig. 52. *Toys, including a baby rattle, a horse on wheels, a top, two dolls, a clay dog, miniature furniture and a toy weaver's comb (KM 7692, KM 7501, KM 7571, KM 3323, KM 7494, KM 6911, KM 26412, KM 3648, KM 22213, KM 10019 and KM 3852a–c; Kelsey Museum photograph by Sue Webb).*

be baked, into the oven and a vent projected from the bottom. Sometimes insulation was provided by building walls of sundried brick around the terracotta oven walls.[43] With the heat of the oven contained, other chores could be done in the courtyard while bread was being baked. Among other things, these would have included the care of household animals. Feeding troughs, roofed mangers and pens attest that the activities of the kitchen and the farm-

yard were normally carried on side by side. Only in the larger homes were there separate courtyards for each activity.

Amid the labors of the day, the engaging presence of children is revealed by the toys they left behind. Infants were amused by rattles made of pebbles encased in a pocket of woven palm or of sticks of wood laced together with string. Toddlers played with pull-toys—wooden horses and birds on

Fig. 53. Two pairs of dice and a small cylindrical box made of bone (KM 21885, KM 22745, KM 22782 and KM 22765–66; Kelsey Museum photograph by Fred Anderegg).

wheels—while somewhat older siblings fashioned their own little animals in clay. Many dolls were cut from flat pieces of wood, and others were made of rags. Some of the rag dolls were even given human hair and removable hooded cloaks.[44] With miniature stools, reading stands and lamps, children provided for their dolls the familiar comforts of home. Tiny clay pots, mortars and amphoras along with diminutive weavers' combs and carpenters' mallets show that children were eager to imitate adults as they went about their daily chores. A small papyrus booklet makes clear that the desire to read and write was instilled in the very young, and wax tablets used by older children for their lessons provide a glimpse of the methods by which these skills were learned. A letter from the Ptolemaic period, sent by two girls to their younger sisters, offers an intimate view of youngsters in a Graeco-Egyptian home:

Fig. 54. Decorative niche in House C119 is thought to have served as a shrine for household gods (Kelsey Museum Archives, 812).

Apollonia and Eupons to Rhasion and Demarion their sisters, greeting. If you are well it is good, we too are well. Please light a lamp for the shrines and spread the cushions. Be diligent at your lessons, and don't worry about Mother; she is getting on fine now. And expect us. Good-bye. P.S. And don't play in the courtyard, but keep good indoors. And look after Titoa and Sphairon.[45]

The letter also reveals that children were taught to honor the gods and to maintain their household shrines, a tradition of worship in the home that reached far back into both the Egyptian and the Graeco-Roman past. In the wealthier houses of Karanis wall niches used for this purpose were often ornamented with an elaborately molded frame. Images of the deities were sometimes painted on the interior walls, and small sacred sculptures in stone, bronze or clay were probably placed inside. Before such shrines, in the flickering light of oil lamps, cushions would have been spread and offerings made to the divine protectors of the family and home.

[1] Husselman, 1979, 29-31.

[2] This arrangement is unlike that of the New Kingdom city of El-Amarna where houses were clustered together and shared facilities such as courtyards. In one instance at El-Amarna five courtyards were shared among eleven houses. See Kemp, 133-34.

[3] Husselman, 1979, 38-39.

[4] Husselman, 1979, 9-30; Boak and Peterson, 2-5 and 39-40.

[5] Johnson, 1936, 256-57.

[6] Youtie and Pearl, 1944, 21 (P. Mich. inv. 2977).

[7] Husselman, 1979, 35.

[8] Johnson, 1936, 330-31 and 360-64; Husselman, 1979, 33.

[9] See Husselman, 1979, 33-36 on Karanis houses; for an explanation of this technique in Egypt in general see Petrie, 1938, 10-12.

[10] Boak and Peterson, 23-27; Husselman, 1979, 37-39.

[11] Husselman, 1979, 44-46.

[12] Ibid., 40-43.

[13] Ibid., 35-36.

[14] Baker, 114.

[15] Wanscher, 11; Baker, 127-34.

[16] Richter, 66, discusses the advantages of three legs in reference to Greek tables.

[17] Egypt's Golden Age, 65; Baker, 150; Richter, 66.

[18] For lightweight Egyptian tables see Baker, 114 and 150; for Roman tables see Richter, 110.

[19] Pliny NH, VII,56.198, comments on the invention of the lathe. The use of the lathe in Egypt prior to Roman influence has been debated. See Lucas, 424-25, 449-50; Aldred in Singer et al., 702; Baker, 303; Wanscher, 15. For turned legs of beds, see Baker, 144.

[20] Youtie and Winter, 32-33 (P.Mich. inv. 5390). Although beds were sent to Karanis, no examples were found by the excavators. Because beds were regarded as valuable possessions (Egypt's Golden Age, 65), it is likely that they would have been taken along when the residents ultimately abandoned the town.

[21] Youtie and Winter, 32-33 (P.Mich. inv. 5390).

[22] Root, 20; Harden, 155-66.

[23] Shier, 1978, passim.

[24] Boak and Peterson, 29-30.

[25] For storage below stairways, Husselman, 1979, 47. Occasionally there was one niche above another, both positioned below the windows. See Boak and Peterson, 29-30.

[26] Boak and Peterson, 29-30.

[27] Found in House C61.

[28] Petrie, 1927, 36 and 45-47; Aldred in Singer et al., 694-95.

[29] Egypt's Golden Age, 65.

[30] For a discussion of the containers to store kohl, see Egypt's Golden Age, 216-17.

[31] Forbes in Singer et al., 292-93.

[32] Typical of Roman influence, Petrie, 1927, 24; Egypt's Golden Age, 198.

[33] Egypt's Golden Age, 197.

[34] Egypt's Golden Age, 133-39; Crowfoot in Singer et al., 422.

[35] Egypt's Golden Age, 133-39.

[36] Youtie and Winter, 24 (P.Mich. inv. 5391).

[37] Bellah, 11-13.

[38] Art of the Ancient Weaver, 5-13.

[39] Bellah, 12-13; Petrie, 1917, 39.

[40] For a description of how a Theban mill operates, see Robinson and Graham, 326-30.

[41] Boak and Peterson, 66.

[42] Husselman, 1971, 71-72 (P. Mich. inv. 6038).

[43] Boak and Peterson, 35-36; Husselman, 1979, 49.

[44] Lindsay, 52; Shier, 1949, 61. For comparisons between Egyptian and Roman toys, see Petrie 1927, 58-62.

[45] Bell, 94 (P.Athen. 60). This letter is not from Karanis.

THE TEMPLES AND THE GODS

The people of Karanis inhabited an environment that reflected their religious preoccupations at every turn. The imposing stone walls of the North and South Temples proclaimed the central role of the public cults in the life of the town. In addition, images of the deities, amulets, votives and equipment used in the celebration of religious rites were to be found in even the most intimate quarters, constantly reminding one of the ever-present gods. The names of many of the deities are recorded in papyrus documents, and a few are inscribed in stone. In all, about twenty-seven divinities are known. Of these, approximately half belonged to the indigenous Egyptian pantheon and half to that of the Greeks. Together these deities, many of whom claimed special jurisdiction over the fecundity of the earth, present a picture of a religious life typical of agrarian communities throughout Egypt in Graeco-Roman times.[1] Not until late antiquity did Christianity make significant inroads into the domains of the ancient gods of the land.

The Cult of the Crocodile

Among the cults of Karanis more is known about that of the crocodile god, Sobek, than any other. Familiar to the Greeks as Souchos, the crocodile, although not worshipped everywhere in Egypt, had held sway in the Fayum since earliest Dynastic times.[2] His cult was centered in Shedyet (Crocodilopolis) but many locales in this region maintained temples in his honor.[3] In the two known temples of Karanis, Souchos was worshipped in three guises—as Pnepheros, Petesouchos and Soknopaios.[4]

Fig. 55. Outer pylon of the North Temple, with a view toward the high altar at the rear of the building (Kelsey Museum Archives, 5.1644).

The powers of the crocodile god were thought to have extended to the very creation of the world. Lake Moeris, in the Fayum, was regarded as the primeval ocean (Nun) of ancient myth wherein all forms of life originated.[5] It was at Shedyet, according to myth, that the primordial mound arose out of the waters of this ocean, and life appeared on the earth for the first time. The crocodile, which emerged silently and mysteriously from the waters of the lakes and river, could be likened to

Fig. 56. A Greek inscription over the main doorway of the South Temple names the crocodile gods Pnepheros and Petesouchos (Kelsey Museum Archives, 5.1808).

Fig. 57. Part of a mummified crocodile found in the inner sanctuary of the North Temple at Karanis (Kelsey Museum Archives, 5.1692).

When anyone, be he Egyptian or stranger, is known to have been carted off by a crocodile or drowned by the river itself, such a one must by all means be embalmed and tended as fairly as may be and buried in a sacred coffin by the townsmen of the place where he is cast up; nor may his kinfolk or his friends touch him, but his body is deemed something more than human, and is handled and buried by the priests of the Nile themselves.[7]

The priests of the crocodile cult at Karanis would have been schooled in such age-old theological tenets and myths, but whether the cosmic significance of the god was understood by the average person in Graeco-Roman times is perhaps doubtful. Indeed, accounts dating to the Roman period suggest that, by and large, the divinity of the crocodile had come to be understood in more concrete terms.

Diodorus of Sicily, who wrote in the first century

the primeval mound and was thus believed to embody the elemental powers of creation.[6] Although a treacherous creature, it was considered a benefactor of the land, analogous to the Nile itself whose threatening floodwaters nonetheless ensured the perpetuity of life. Writing in the fifth century BC, Herodotus confirms the Egyptians' traditional belief in the elemental power of this beast and its ability to transform human beings into something approaching the divine:

AD, expressed skepticism at the notion of the deification of crocodiles:

. . . a subject regarding which most men are entirely at a loss to explain how, when these beasts eat the flesh of men, it ever became the law to honour like the gods creatures of the most revolting habits.[8]

He found that Egyptians themselves varied in their views of why the crocodile was held sacred. Some claimed that it ensured the safety of the country since foreign robbers were prevented from crossing the river into Egypt because of the great number of crocodiles in it. Others explained that the crocodile had saved an early king from his own vicious dogs by carrying him on its back to the other side of Lake Moeris and that on this account the king commanded the inhabitants of the region to pay homage to the beast.[9] Plutarch, writing at about the same time, found the reasons for deification to reside in the character and habits of the crocodile itself:

. . . it is said to be the only tongueless creature and thus a likeness of God. For the divine reason does not need a voice, and

> passing on a noiseless path,
> Guides mortal things aright;
> (Eur. Tro. 887–88)

and they say that the crocodile, alone of creatures that live in the water, has covering its eyes a smooth transparent membrane which comes down from its forehead, so that it sees without being seen to do so, which is true of the highest God.[10]

Moreover, both Plutarch and Pliny the Elder maintained that the crocodile was a prophet of the annual inundation, since the females, sensing the levels of the coming flood, would lay their eggs just beyond the anticipated high water mark.[11] Further, according to Plutarch:

They lay sixty eggs and hatch them in so many days and those who live longest live for this number of years, which is the primary measure for those concerned with heavenly phenomena.[12]

Temples and Ceremonies

While it may not be possible from these varying accounts to know how the ordinary citizens of Karanis regarded the crocodile god, some idea of how they worshipped this divinity may be gained both from the architecture of the North and South Temples and from related sanctuaries at other towns in the Fayum. Like all Egyptian temples, these sacred structures were the abodes of the god, in which, given the proper invocations, he would appear to his devotees. As Henri Frankfort, a prominent historian of Egyptian art and thought, has articulated this concept,

. . . the temple, in Egypt, was a place of power. The gods were immanent in nature, and hence difficult to localize. The temple cast a spell, as it were, on a given spot where divinities might be approached.[13]

The form of the temple building was prescribed by Egyptian religious tradition, and scholars of Egyptian architecture have interpreted its plan as a cosmic metaphor.[14] Approached along a causeway, open air courts precede a series of enclosed rooms

Fig. 58. Roman period ostracon showing a sacred crocodile on a litter in a temple sanctuary (O. Mich. inv. 4270 [= O.Mich. I 97]). Reproduced with the permission of the Papyrology Collection, Graduate Library, The University of Michigan.

which gradually diminish in size, an arrangement which provided an ideal model symbolic of the universe at the beginning of time. Even in the use of stone for the temple walls, the permanence of this universe was proclaimed.

At the South Temple of Karanis one may observe this typical arrangement. A paved walk leads to a colonnaded courtyard which like all such temple courtyards, symbolized the primordial marsh. The columns represented the plants of the marsh but, by rendering them in stone, their perishable nature had been overcome and their essence preserved. Beyond the courtyard lay the temple building proper. The first and largest chamber gave access to a smaller room which served as a vestibule to

Fig. 59. South Temple, eastern façade, viewed across the forecourt; the gateway at left is shown in figure 62 (Kelsey Museum Archives, 5.3311).

Fig. 60. Interior chambers of the South Temple; the platform of the high altar is visible at the back (Kelsey Museum Archives, 5.3363).

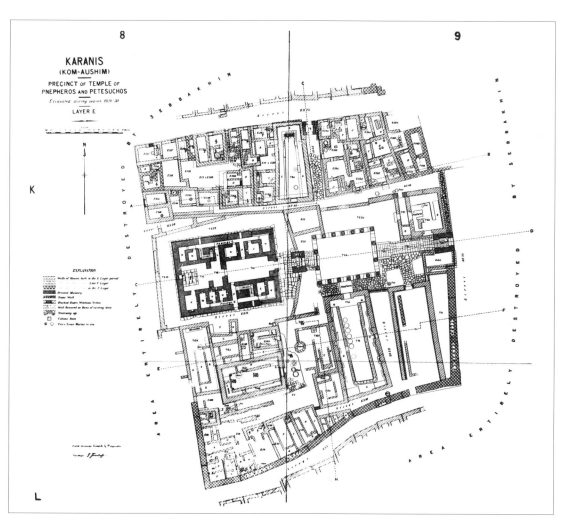

Fig. 61. South Temple complex. The temple and colonnaded court are flanked by a variety of ceremonial buildings (after Peterson in Boak, 1933, plan III) .

the innermost chamber which housed the sacred shrine. In this sanctuary, a high platform or altar represented the primeval mound.[15] Here, probably in dim torchlight or in darkness broken only by rays of the sun entering through the doorway, sacred rites were performed by the priests to invoke an epiphany of the god.[16]

We can do no more than speculate upon the nature of the various duties and ceremonies performed by the priests of the North and South Temples at Karanis, for no records of them have come down to us from the town. Herodotus informs us of some of the practices of the crocodile cult both at Thebes and in the Fayum in the fifth century BC, which included the elaborate care of the live animals as well as their mummification after death:

There, in every place one crocodile is kept, trained to be tame; they put ornaments of glass and gold on its ears and bracelets on its forefeet, provide for it special food and offerings, and give the creatures the best of treatment while they live; after death the crocodiles are embalmed and buried in sacred coffins.[17]

Strabo, writing in the first century BC of his visit to Crocodilopolis, confirms some of the observations of Herodotus. He reports that the tamed crocodile, called Souchos, was kept in a lake on the temple grounds and was fed grain, pieces of meat, wine and milk mixed with honey brought by foreigners who came to see the divine creature.[18]

At Karanis there is no evidence to indicate that live crocodiles were kept within the temple precincts. However, numerous crocodile mummies which had been buried together were discovered, and certain

Fig. 62. Gateway to the banquet hall of the South Temple, constructed during the reign of Vespasian (Kelsey Museum Archives, 5.3399).

architectural features of the temples attest that mummified animals were used in the temple ceremonies. Deep niches in the inner walls of the vestibules of both the North and the South Temples evidently were used to store the mummies, which were brought

out on biers for display upon the high altar. Behind the altars of both temples are recesses into which the ends of the biers may have been placed.[19] Similar architectural features are found in other temples of the crocodile god in the Fayum.[20]

Very likely, the ceremony performed by the priests included the "unveiling, aspersing, censing, and anointing" of the mummified god, and the presentation of offerings.[21] Animals would have been sacrificed and their burnt flesh presented to the god. Probably the remains of the sacrificial offering would have been consumed by the priests at a sacred banquet, possibly in the company of wealthy citizens of the town.[22] In the South Temple precinct, a large hall was constructed for this purpose during the reign of the Emperor Vespasian (AD 69–79). Other specially equipped rooms within the temple complex must also have served particular purposes. One room held a large vat, possibly used for lustral baths,[23] but the function of others which were provided with water vessels and drains remains obscure.[24]

During the ceremonies conducted within the temple proper, the duties of the priests probably included the presentation of petitions on behalf of lay devotees who were not allowed within the hallowed shrine. The daily concerns of the average person were submitted to the god in writing in the hope of obtaining advice through an oracular response.[25] A document from the year AD 6 addressed to Soknopaios, exemplifies such petitions:

To the most great and mighty god Soknopaios, from Asclepiades son of Arius. Is it granted me to marry

Fig. 63. North Temple. View of the interior rooms and altar platform (Kelsey Museum Archives, 5.1643).

Tapetheus daughter of Marres; will she certainly be none other's wife? Show me and give me authoritative answer to this written inquiry. . . . Formerly Tapetheus was Horion's wife.[26]

A peculiar detail of the construction of the altars of the North and South Temples may indicate that provision had been made for the utterance of oracles. Within each altar is a small chamber which can be entered through a low opening along one side. It would have been possible for a priest to remain hidden inside the altar while delivering the appropriate responses on behalf of the god.[27] Along both sides of the South Temple, several houses were discovered within the precinct wall which may have served the needs of such worshippers, some of whom might have traveled from a distance. Several rooms are provided with benches built along the

Fig. 64. Procession in honor of the crocodile god. Copy of a wall painting in the Temple of Pnepheros at Theadelphia (after Breccia, 1926, pl. LXIV, 3).

37

walls where one could rest until it was time to enter the temple and await the outcome of one's petition to the god.[28]

At various times throughout the year, during religious festivals, the image of the god was taken out of his temple and was carried in procession through the town. Frescoes depicting a procession of the crocodile god were discovered at the temple of Pnepheros at Theadelphia in the Fayum.[29] The noted Egyptologist, Cyril Aldred, conjures up a lively image of what the emotional climate must have been like on such an occasion:

His image, suitably veiled or hidden in the primeval shrine, was placed on a litter and carried on the shoulders of his priests in procession. . . . As the cortege went on its circuit amid the shouts of the populace, the chanting of the temple choir, the blowing of trumpets, the beating of drums, the rattling of sistra, and the burning of incense, emotions rose to a pitch of hysteria, and in such a frenzy the moment was ripe for the god to intervene in the affairs of man by giving oracular answers to suppliants by the spasmodic movements of the litter and the shoulders of its bearers. So the morale of true believers was sustained by the presence of the god in their midst, by the evidence of his divine power, and by his concern in their everyday affairs.[30]

The Wider Pantheon

Such ceremonies and festivals would not have been restricted to the cult of the crocodile at Karanis. Although the portal inscriptions of the South Temple name only Pnepheros and Petesouchos, images of several gods found within the South

Fig. 65. Harpocrates, the child-god, holds a pottery vessel symbolic of abundance (KM 6464; Kelsey Museum photograph by Fred Anderegg).

Temple complex and of two more deities in the North suggest that the crocodile gods shared their venerable abodes. A case in point is that of the youthful god, Harpocrates, no fewer than eight images of whom derive from the South Temple complex.[31]

The cult of Harpocrates flourished in Egypt during the Roman era; and we know from three notices in the tax rolls that there was a priest of his cult at Karanis.[32] Moreover, many additional images of Harpocrates, in paintings as well as terracotta figurines, were found in the granaries and houses throughout the town, indicating that the god was highly esteemed in the private sphere as well.[33] The popularity of Harpocrates in agrarian communities like Karanis may be attributed, in large part, to his close association with the fertility of the earth. Harpocrates, or Horus the Child, was thought to have been conceived by Isis after the murder and dismemberment of her husband, Osiris, by his wicked brother, Seth. According to the well-known myth, Isis traveled over the whole land gathering up the parts of the body of Osiris, and then magically restored him to life. Thereafter, Osiris reigned in the underworld as lord of life after death. This myth, central to Egyptian religion in all periods, was readily related by ordinary people to the cycle of the agricultural year. In fact, this was so common that Plutarch speaks disparagingly of

. . . the many boring people who find pleasure in associating the activities of these gods with the seasonal changes of the atmosphere or with the growth, sowing and ploughing of crops, and who say that Osiris is being buried when the corn is sown and hidden in the earth, and that he lives again and reappears when it begins to sprout.[34]

As regards the infant god Harpocrates, Plutarch goes on to report the generally held belief that Isis

. . . at the winter solstice gave birth to Harpocrates, imperfect and prematurely born, amid plants that burgeoned and sprouted before their season (and so they bring to him as offering the first-fruits of growing lentils). . . .[35]

Fig. 66. Isis. The torso of this marble statue was found in the inner court of the North Temple (KM 8196 and KM 25941, joined; Kelsey Museum photograph by Fred Anderegg).

Fig. 67. Soknopaios with a reptilian body and the head of a hawk; from the inner court of the North Temple (KM 25752; Kelsey Museum photograph by Fred Anderegg).

Fig. 68. Isis holding Harpocrates; adjoining the mother and child is the Thracian rider-god Heron in House B50 (Kelsey Museum Archives, 5.2159).

In keeping with the humble faith of the farmer, many of the terracotta figurines of Harpocrates from Karanis show the young god with such symbols of the land's fertility as cornucopiae and pottery jars. Harpocrates probably also appealed to the masses of people as a patron deity of childhood and as an instructive model to youth.[36] According to the myth, this child of Isis and Osiris grew up to avenge the death of his father and so could be held as an ideal of filial virtue.

In the Roman period the cult of Harpocrates was often merged with those of other gods, including that of the crocodile, and perhaps it was in this context that his cult was administered at Karanis.[37] Among the images of Harpocrates from the South Temple area is a fragment of a magical cippus of a type which depicts the young god standing on the backs of two crocodiles. In this guise he was considered to be the slayer of the menacing beasts rather than their divine ally.[38] The cippus thus suggests aspects of ambiguity in the Egyptian worship of certain animals, which, in reality, they had good reason to fear.

Multiple images of Isis found at Karanis attest that devotion to her cult was also widespread in the town, and the tax rolls twice mention her priests.[39] A marble torso of her found in the inner court of the North Temple, along with two images of Soknopaios, suggests that her official cult was located there. Isis was revered throughout the Roman world not only as a model of marital and maternal devotion but also as a goddess of supreme and all-encompassing powers.[40] In the Fayum, at Soknopaiou

Nesos, her cult was joined to that of Soknopaios, and it seems likely that this was the case at Karanis as well.[41] Appropriately, in the guise of Soknopaios, the crocodile god took on aspects of the character of Horus, the goddess's son. Although represented with a reptilian body, he was given the head of the Horus hawk.[42]

One of the most striking portrayals of Isis to have survived Karanis is a wall painting from a private house in which she is shown holding the infant Harpocrates to her breast.[43] It is easy to understand how strongly the maternal aspect of this deity would have appealed to the women of the town. Only the ugly dwarf-god, Bes, patron of women in child-birth, seems to have rivaled Isis in the domestic sphere, judging from the great numbers of amulets of him that were found. Isis was also worshipped at Karanis in a specifically agrarian form, identified with the cobra goddess, Thermouthis, whose particular charge was to protect the harvested grain. Sculptures of Isis-Thermouthis with serpentine tail, along with votive footprints dedicated to her, were found in private dwellings, where they were probably originally displayed in household shrines.[44]

Osiris, the third member of the mythical triad, is represented among the finds from Karanis by only two terracotta figurines, one of which comes from the South Temple where his cult could have been linked with that of the crocodile gods.[45] Worship of Osiris may, however, have been overshadowed by that of Sarapis, the Graeco-Egyptian god whose cult was encouraged by the Ptolemies as a means of integrating the religious beliefs of the native Egyptians

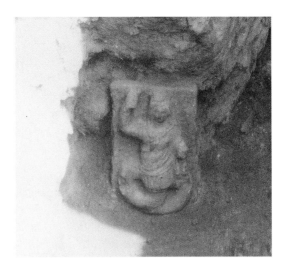

Fig. 69. Isis-Thermouthis. Limestone relief as discovered in House 5021F. The goddess is depicted with the tail of a cobra (KM 25751; Kelsey Museum Archives, 5.1690).

with those of the immigrant Greeks. The persona of Sarapis first emerged from that of Osiris, who was worshipped at Memphis in the guise of the Apis-bull (Osir-apis); but under the Ptolemies, Sarapis also acquired the characteristic powers of three Greek divinities: Hades, god of the underworld, Asklepios, god of health, and Zeus, chief among the Olympians.[46] As a god of fecundity and resurrection, Sarapis enjoyed great popularity within Egypt in Roman times. His cult, like that of Isis, spread throughout the Roman world. The countenance of Sarapis has survived in several fine sculptures from Karanis, and there is a partially preserved

Fig. 70. Osiris. This terracotta figurine, which shows the god as a bust-length mummy, was found in House 11 (KM 6478; Kelsey Museum photograph by Fred Anderegg).

image of him enthroned among other deities in a wall painting from a private house.[47] The official center of his cult at Karanis was very likely located in the North Temple, along with those of Isis and Soknopaios. Here a large fire altar bearing the head of Sarapis-Zeus-Amon-Helios, as the god was commonly called in Roman times, was found in the rubble which had tumbled from the outer court of the sanctuary.[48]

In addition to the crocodile nome god and the divine triad of Isis, Sarapis, and Harpocrates, many other deities, both Greek and Egyptian, claimed devotees in the town. Often it is not possible to tell whether these gods had separate cults, for the tendency to identify counterparts within each pantheon was common since the Greeks first settled in Egypt.[49] Herodotus gives a scattered account of the various equivalents that were known in his day, and Plutarch, writing more than six centuries later, confirms that the great Egyptian gods were known by other names in other lands. Plutarch was concerned that people

. . . preserve the gods as our common heritage and do not make them the peculiar property of the Egyptians. Nor should they comprehend under these names merely the Nile and only the land which the Nile waters, nor speak of marshes and lotus-flowers as the only work of the gods. By so doing they would take these great gods from the rest of mankind, who have no Nile or Buto or Memphis. But Isis and the gods related to her belong to all men and are known to them; even though they have not long since learnt to call some of them by their Egyptian names, they have understood and honoured the power of each god from the beginnings.[50]

Fig. 71. Fire altar with the head of Sarapis-Zeus-Amon-Helios from the outer court of the North Temple (Kelsey Museum Archives, 5.1606).

An especially striking example of the combining of cults at Karanis is found in the wall painting from a private house, mentioned above. Here the Greek Eleusinian deities, Persephone, Demeter

Fig. 72. Aphrodite. Bronze statue of the Greek goddess of love found in House 418 (KM 10728; Kelsey Museum photograph by Fred Anderegg)

41

Fig. 73. Nilos, the river god of Egypt, shown propped against a partially preserved cornucopia and sphinx (KM 25747, KM 25869 and KM 25879, joined; Kelsey Museum photograph by Fred Anderegg).

Fig. 74. Topos graffiti on the walls of the North Temple may have marked the spaces of individual merchants' stalls (Kelsey Museum Archives, 5.2249).

and Triptolemus, stand alongside the thrones of Isis (?) and Sarapis in the company of several other divinities whose identities are uncertain.[51] On the adjacent wall, a nude female figure very likely represents Aphrodite, a goddess who was honored particularly in the private sphere, either in purely Greek form or identified with Hathor, Isis or another Egyptian counterpart. Numerous statuettes of Aphrodite were found at Karanis, and it is tempting to think that these may have belonged to young brides. In Roman times, a typical dowry would have included an image of the goddess of love.[52]

Sculpted representations of the Greek divinities Herakles, Eros, Priapus and possibly Apollo have survived while Dionysus, Hades, Moira and Zeus are only mentioned in the papyri, the last three in an epigram of a Greek youth.[53] From the Egyptian

pantheon of gods whose presence is known from the archeological remains are Nefertum and Nilos, the latter often closely identified with the crocodile god of the nome.[54] Imhotep (who was identified with Asklepios), Anubis (the counterpart of Hermes as guide to the underworld), and Apis are named in the papyri, but about their worship at Karanis little more is known. Most of these gods may have been honored at household shrines, while for some the written testimony suggests that actual sanctuaries were maintained.[55] Possibly there were other temples in the town which were destroyed by the *sebbakhin*, although if they were made of stone they would have required great effort to dismantle. More likely, the South and North Temples were host to many gods, as was common in Egypt especially in Graeco-Roman times.

Temples in Prosperity and Decline

In any case, the public temples surely had a dominant place in the religious life of the town, and they no doubt served as the focus of much of its economic life as well. As in most Egyptian towns in the Roman period, market places and craftsmen's shops probably clustered close by the walls of the sacred precincts. In fact the walls of the North Temple are incised with graffiti, repeating the Greek word *topos* (place or site) at varying intervals. Some have thought these to signify a dedication of some sort, but one scholar believes that they marked the spaces allotted to individual merchants for their stalls.[56] Further, while there is no certain evidence to indicate that the priests themselves engaged in the sale of goods in the manner of private businessmen, there can be no question that at Karanis, as at many other towns of this period, certain trades were attached to the temples, probably to produce income. Papyri from Karanis attest that sheep

shearers, and wool merchants and possibly fullers, operated under the aegis of the temple.[57] Commercial enterprises of this sort undoubtedly produced a substantial portion of the revenue that went toward maintaining the temples and their staffs and toward paying for the supplies needed for various cult ceremonies and festivals. Some of the items commonly required for these purposes included:

. . . robes for the gods and spice and ointments for sacrifices, the care of cult animals . . . , embalming of the sacred crocodile, . . . Oil . . . for annointing and for illumination, and wine . . . for purification and other ceremonial uses.[58]

At many towns in Egypt income was derived from the leasing of lands owned by the temples—lands which were often acquired by gift or bequest. It is not known whether this was the case at Karanis, but the tax rolls do record the payment of the *gera*, apparently levied on offerings received by the priests.[59] Other forms of private donation are also known. An inscription from the South Temple precinct names one Apollonius, *sitologus* (superintendent) of the granaries, as the donor of a gateway on the north side of the precinct, a gift which he made in the reign of the Emperor Commodus (AD 180–192).[60]

Much of the revenue collected by an Egyptian temple in the Roman era was paid out in taxation. In addition to the *gera* on offerings, the priests at Karanis paid the *epistatikon*, a levy which, in Ptolemaic times, may have covered the salary of a government agent. The Roman administration continued

Fig. 75. *Christian symbols on a platter, a lamp and amulets bear witness to the new religion at Karanis (KM 4767, KM 7145, KM 7561, KM 8495, KM 21936 and KM 24251; Kelsey Museum photograph by Sue Webb).*

to collect the tax but evidently did not retain the agent.[61] Other taxes imposed by the Roman government on Egyptian temples took the form of initiation fees and the sale of priestly offices. Although the priesthood was hereditary in Egypt, initiation fees were collected when one entered into any of the offices in the hierarchy.[62] Among the posts sold to the highest bidder were those of prophet, *stolistes*, pastophoros, palm bearer, and image bearer. No record of these transactions survives from Karanis, but one can be sure that the practice obtained here as throughout the province.

It was common in the third century AD for priests to abandon their posts, and with their defection the local cults fell into decline.[63] At Karanis, the North and South Temples, which had been in steady use since the early Roman period, were deserted at about this time.[64] The reason most often cited for the abandonment of the old gods is the spread of Christianity. By the fourth century in Egypt, monastic communities, which had first developed on Egyptian soil, were well established. In both a religious and an economic sense, they had supplanted the traditions of the pagan shrines.[65] Evidence for the rising strength of Christianity among the townspeople of Karanis does not come from places of worship. It emerges rather from numerous objects of household use such as pottery, lamps and textiles which came to be ornamented with emblems of the new faith. Many of the imported African Red Slip platters and bowls found at Karanis are impressed with crosses, lambs, or images of saints. Painted vessels show fish, birds, hares and other fauna which had served as symbols of the old religion but were now adapted to the new. Lamps, some in the form of frogs which signified to the ancient Egyptian the fertility goddess, Heqet, became symbols of resurrection to the believer in Christ.[66] Small crosses of bone, wood and colored glass, as well as garment fragments in which the same designs are woven, all attest to the widespread acceptance of Christianity by the people of the town.

The old gods did not disappear without a trace, however. In the third or fourth century school children still practiced writing the names of Egyptian and Greek gods on broken pieces of pottery. One of these may even have been the work of a Jewish child, for the sherd seems to preserve the word "Sabbath" among the names of the gods.[67] In the Christian context such images as that of Isis holding the infant Harpocrates may have been understood as the Virgin and Child, just as the rider-god Heron became the model for many a Christian saint.[68] A century after the temples had fallen into ruin, the majority of the population of Karanis had converted to the new faith, but echoes of the town's pagan past continued to be heard for another hundred years until all life at Karanis ceased.

[1] Rübsam, 98–104; Grenfell, Hunt and Hogarth, 32–34; Shelton, 33–36. See Dunand, 1979, 107–8 for a discussion of fertility gods in an agrarian setting.

[2] Herodotus, II.69; Strabo, 17.1.44–47; Dolzani, 173–74.

[3] Toutain, 12; Habachi, 1955, 108; Kuentz, 1929, 169–70; Kees, 1931, cols. 541–51.

[4] Grenfell, Hunt and Hogarth, 30–35; Boak, 1933, 13–14; Peterson in Boak, 1933, 17–55; Yeivin, 72.

[5] Kees, 1961, 224.

[6] Aldred, 1978, 32–33.

[7] Herodotus, II.90.

[8] Diodorus Siculus, 1.89.1–2.

[9] Ibid., I.89.3.

[10] Plutarch, De Is. et Os., 75.

[11] Plutarch, op. cit.; Pliny, VIII.37.89.

[12] Plutarch, op. cit.

[13] Frankfort, 155.

[14] Frankfort, 150–55; Aldred, 1978, 37–38.

[15] Frankfort, 153.

[16] Peterson in Boak, 1933, 51.

[17] Herodotus, II.69.

[18] Strabo, 17.1.38.

[19] Boak, 1933, 9 and 13; Peterson in Boak, 1933, 52–53.

[20] Breccia, 117.

[21] Aldred, 1978, 57.

[22] For banquets of Sarapis see Bell, 94 and Youtie, 13–27.

[23] Peterson in Boak, 1933, 41. See Herodotus, II.35 on the frequent bathing of priests.

[24] Ibid., 36–38.

[25] Bell, 95; Dolzani, 212.

[26] Bell, 95 (W.Chr. 122). This letter is not from Karanis.

[27] Boak, 1933, 9; Peterson in Boak, 1933, 53.

[28] Peterson in Boak, 1933, 40.

[29] Breccia, 105–6 and 120.

[30] Aldred, 1978, 61–66; see Dunand, 1979, 93–94 for such religious processions.

[31] Gazda et al., Appendix nos. 25, 64, 70, 74, 76, 77, 78, 82.

[32] Dunand, 1975, 162; idem., 1979, 73–87; Witt, 210–21; Youtie and Pearl, 1939, pt. II, p. 140; Rübsam, 98–99; Shelton, 33–34.

[33] Gazda et al, Cat. nos. 22, 49, 63, 64 and Appendix nos. 65–69, 71–73, 75, 79–81.

[34] Plutarch, De Is. et Os., 65.

[35] Ibid.

[36] Gods of Egypt, 33.

[37] Milne, 210–11; Griffiths, 44; Dolzani, 220–24.

[38] Gazda et al., Appendix no. 25; cp. *Gods of Egypt*, nos. 15, 16; Dolzani, 167; Plutarch, *De Is. et Os.*, 19; Griffiths, 346.

[39] Gazda et al., Cat. nos. 24, 26, 52, 65 and Appendix nos. 83–86; Youtie and Pearl, 1939, pt. II, p. 140; Rübsam, 99–100; Shelton, 34.

[40] Dunand, 1973, passim; Witt, passim.

[41] Kees, 1931, col. 558. For Isis and Pnepheros at Theadelphia see Breccia, 120; for Karanis, Boak, 1933, 13–14.

[42] Toutain, 177; Boak, 1933, 13; Kees, 1931, cols. 551–52; Dolzani, 185 and 217; Gazda et al., Cat. nos. 31–32.

[43] Boak and Peterson, p. 34 fig. 49. On the maternal nature of Isis see Dunand, 1979, 60–70.

[44] Gazda et al., pp. 13–14 and Cat. nos. 26 (Isis-Thermouthis) and 34 (footprint); Dunand, 1979, 63–66.

[45] Gazda et al., Appendix nos. 89–90; Kees, 1931, cols. 553–54.

[46] Dunand, 1979, 87–92; idem., 1975, 160–61; idem., 1973, I, 45–66; Brady, 9–12.

[47] Gazda et al., Cat. nos. 28–30, 47, 54; Parlasca, p. 212, pl. 46, 1.

[48] Boak, 1933, 12.

[49] Dunand, 1975, passim.

[50] Plutarch, *De Is. et Os.*, 66.

[51] Parlasca, p. 212, pl. 46, 1.

[52] Gazda et al., Cat. nos. 16–20, 39, 40, 48, Appendix 14; Bell, 87 on dowries; Johnson, 1936, 521 notes a tax on the holy ground of Aphrodite.

[53] Gazda et al., Cat. nos. 21, 23, 27, 41–45; Rübsam, 102–3.

[54] Gazda et al., Cat. nos. 26, 53, Appendix 27.

[55] Rübsam, 98–104.

[56] Yeivin, 78–79; Johnson, 1936, 642.

[57] Johnson, 1936, 642–43; Shelton, 37.

[58] Johnson, 1936, 645.

[59] Johnson, 1936, 640 on lands; idem., 556 on *gera*.

[60] Grenfell, Hunt and Hogarth, 34; Peterson in Boak, 1933, 42.

[61] Johnson, 1936, 562.

[62] Herodotus, 11.40 on hereditary priesthood; Johnson, 1936, 645–46 on sale of offices.

[63] Johnson, 1936, 647.

[64] The North Temple was in use between the early first and mid-third century AD according to Boak, 1933, 14–15; the South Temple site was occupied from the first century BC until the late third or early fourth century AD. See Peterson in Boak, 1933, 20.

[65] Johnson, 1936, 647.

[66] Shier 1978, 24 and 48.

[67] Rübsam, 104. The interpretation of this ostrakon is, however, controversial, as Rübsam points out. [The text (*O.Mich.* I 657), in fact, reads "Sambathis," which is well known as a personal name in Egypt in the Roman period and less likely to be a direct reference to the "Sabbath"–TGW.]

[68] Witt, ch. 20; Bell, 88–89.

SELECT BIBLIOGRAPHY

Classical Authors

All translations cited in the text are taken from editions of The Loeb Classical Library with the exception of Plutarch, for which see J. G. Griffiths, below.

Columella, *De Re Rustica*

Dio Chrysostomus, *Orationes*

Diodorus Siculus, *Bibliotheke*

Herodotus, *The Histories*

Josephus, *Bellum Iudaicum*

Pliny the Elder, *Naturalis Historia*

Plutarch, *De Iside et Osiride*

Seneca, *Epistulae*

Strabo, *Geography*

Varro, *De Re Rustica*

Secondary Sources

Aldred, C. 1978. "The Temple of Dendur," *Bulletin of the Metropolitan Museum of Art* (Summer 1978).

*Allen, F. 1947. *Ports and Happy Havens*. London: Frederick Muller. [Anecdotal account of Karanis excavation on pp. 89–110]

*Allen, M. L. 1985. "The Terracotta Figurines from Karanis: A Study of Technique, Style and Chronology in Fayumic Coroplastics." 3 vols. Ann Arbor: University of Michigan, Ph.D. dissertation.

*Allen, M. L., and T. K. Dix. 1991. *The Beginning of Understanding: Writing in the Ancient World*. Ann Arbor: Kelsey Museum of Archaeology.

*Alston, R. 1995. *Soldier and Society in Roman Egypt: A Social History*. London: Routledge. [Extensive use of Karanis material]
*———. 2002. *The City in Roman and Byzantine Egypt*. London: Routledge.

*Amundsen, L. 1935. *Greek Ostraca in the University of Michigan Collection: Part I, Texts*. University of Michigan Studies, Humanistic Series, vol. 34. Ann Arbor: University of Michigan Press. ["Ostraca from Karanis," pp. 33–181]

Andrews, C. A. R. 1981 *Catalogue of Egyptian Antiquities in the British Museum VI: Jewelry I*. London: British Museum.

The Art of the Ancient Weaver: Textiles from Egypt (4th–12th Century A.D.). 1980. Ann Arbor: Kelsey Museum of Archaeology.

*Auth, S. 1989. [Karanis objects]. In: *Beyond the Pharaohs: Egypt and the Copts in the 2nd to 7th Centuries A.D.*, ed. F. D. Friedman. Providence: Museum of Art, Rhode Island School of Design. [Exhibition catalogue]

*Bagnall, R. S. 1993. *Egypt in Late Antiquity*. Princeton: Princeton University Press.

Baker, H. S. 1966. *Furniture in the Ancient World: Origins and Evolution, 3100–475 B.C.* New York: Macmillan.

Bellah, M. S. 1980. "Agricultural and Carpentry Implements from Karanis" (unpublished paper: Kelsey Museum of Archaeology).

Bell, H. I. 1948. "Popular Religion in Graeco-Roman Egypt," *Journal of Egyptian Archaeology* 34:82–97.

*Bietak, M. 1970. Karanis. *Archiv für Orientforschung* 23:208.

Boak, A. E. R. 1933. *Karanis: The Temple, Coin Hoards, Botanical and Zoölogical Reports, Seasons 1924–31*. University of Michigan Humanistic Series, vol. 30. Ann Arbor: University of Michigan Press.
———. 1944–45. "Early Byzantine Tax Receipts from Egypt," *Byzantion* 17:16–28.
———. 1947, "Tax Collecting in Byzantine Egypt," *Journal of Roman Studies* 37:24–33.

Boak, A. E. B., and E. E. Peterson. 1931. *Karanis: Topographical and Architectural Report of Excavations during the Seasons 1924–28*. University of Michigan Humanistic Series, vol. 25. Ann Arbor: University of Michigan Press.

*Boak, A. E. R., and H. C. Youtie. 1960. *The Archive of Aurelius Isidorus in the Egyptian Museum, Cairo and the University of Michigan (P.Cair.Isidor.).* Ann Arbor: University of Michigan Press. [Archive found at Karanis around 1923]

*Bowman, A. K. 1996. *Egypt after the Pharaohs 332 BC–AD 642,* rev. ed. Berkeley: University of California Press.

Brady, T. A. 1935. *The Reception of the Egyptian Cults by the Greeks (330–30 B.C.),* The University of Missouri Studies, X, 1. Columbia: University of Missouri Press.

Breccia, E. 1926. *Monuments de l'Égypte gréco-romaine, I, 2.* Bergamo: Istituto italiano d'arti grafiche.

Butler, O. F. 1930. "Report of the Museum of Classical Archaeology," *Report of the President of the University of Michigan, 1928–29* (Ann Arbor) 3–12.

*Davoli, P. 1998. *L'archeologia urbana nell Fayyum di età ellenistica e romana.* Mission Congiunta delle Università di Bologna e di Lecce in Egitto, Monografie 1. Bologna: Generoso Procaccini. [See especially pp. 73–116]

Dolzani, C. 1961. *Il Dio Sobk.* Memorie: Accademia nazionale dei Lincei, ser. VIII, vol. X, fasc. 4. Rome: Accademia Lincei.

Domning, D. P. 1977. "Some Examples of Egyptian Ropework," *Chronique d'Égypte* 52:49–61.

Drower, M. S. 1982. "The Early Years," *Excavating in Egypt: The Egypt Exploration Society 1882–1982,* ed. T. G. H. James, 9–36. London: British Museum Publications.

Dunand, F. 1973. *Le culte d'Isis dans le bassin oriental de la Méditerranée I–III.* Études préliminaires aux religions orientaux dans l'empire romain 26. Leiden: E. J. Brill.
——. 1975. "Les syncrétismes dans la religion de l'Égypte romaine," *Les syncrétismes dans les religions de l'antiquité,* Colloque de Besançon (22–23 Octobre 1973), eds. E Dunand and P Lévèque, 152–85. (Études préliminaires aux religions orientaux dans l'empire romain 46. Leiden: E. J. Brill.
——. 1979. *Religion populaire en Égypte romaine; Les terres cuites isiaques du Musée du Caire.* Études preliminaries aux religions orientaux dans l'empire Romain 76. Leiden: E. J. Brill.

Duncan-Jones, R. P. 1976. "The Price of Wheat in Roman Egypt under the Principate," *Chiron* 6:241–62.

Egypt's Golden Age: The Art of Living in the New Kingdom 1558–1085 B.C. 1982. Boston: Museum of Fine Arts.

*El-Nassery, S. A. A. 1975. "A New Roman Hoard from Karanis," *Bulletin de l'Institut Français d'Archéologie Orientale* 75:183–202.

*El-Nassery, S. A. A., G. Wagner and G. Castel. 1976. "Un grand bain gréco-romain à Karanis: Fouilles de l'Université du Caire (1972–75)," *Bulletin de l'Institut Français d'Archéologie Orientale* 76:231–75.

Frankfort, H. 1961. *Ancient Egyptian Religion: An Interpretation.* New York: Harper & Row.

*Frankfurter, D. T. 1998. *Religion in Roman Egypt: Assimilation and Resistance.* Princeton: Princeton University Press.

Fraser, P. M. 1960. "Two Studies on the Cult of Sarapis in the Hellenistic World," *Opuscula Atheniensia* 3:1–55.
——. 1967. "Current Problems Concerning the Early History of the Cult of Sarapis," *Opuscula Atheniensia* 7:23–45.

*Gagos, T. 2001. "The University of Michigan Collection: Current Trends and Future Perspectives." In: *Atti del XXII Congresso Internazionale di Papirologia, Firenze,* I:511–37. Florence Istituto Papirologico "G. Vitelli." [Note especially pp. 520–25: "The Challenge of Karanis: Papyrology Meets Archaeology"]

Gazda, E. K., et al. 1978. *Guardians of the Nile: Sculptures from Karanis in the Fayoum (c. 250 B.C.–A.D. 450).* Ann Arbor: Kelsey Museum of Archaeology.

Geremek, H. 1969. *Karanis: Communauté rurale de l'Égypte romaine au IIe–IIIe siècle de notre ère.* Archiwum Filologiczne, vol. 17. Wroclaw: Zaklad Narodowy Imienia Ossolinskich Wydawnictwo Polskiej Akademii Nauk.

Gods of Egypt in the Graeco-Roman Period, eds. A. Haeckl and K. Spelman. 1977. Ann Arbor: Kelsey Museum of Archaeology.

Goodspeed, E. J. 1902. "Karanis Papyri," *University of Chicago Studies in Classical Philology* 3:1–66.

Grenfell, B. P., A. S. Hunt, D. G. Hogarth and J. G. Milne. 1900. *Fayûm Towns and Their Papyri.* London: Egypt Exploration Fund. [Includes papyri and account of survey of Karanis ("Kom Oushim")]

Griffiths, J. G., ed. and trans. 1970. *Plutarch's de Iside et Osiride, with Introduction and Commentary.* Swansea: University of Wales Press.

Haatvedt, R. A., and E. E. Peterson. 1964. *Coins from Karanis,* ed. E. Husselman. Ann Arbor: Kelsey Museum of Archaeology.

Habachi, L. 1936. "Une 'Vaste Salle' d'Amenemhat III à Kiman-Farès (Fayum)," *Annales du Service des antiquités de l'Égypte* 37:85–95.

——. 1955. "A Strange Monument of the Ptolemaic Period from Crocodilopolis," *Journal of Egyptian Archaeology* 41:106–11.

Harden, D. B. 1936. *Roman Glass from Karanis Found by the University of Michigan Archaeological Expedition in Egypt, 1924–29.* University of Michigan Humanistic Series, vol. 41. Ann Arbor: University of Michigan Press.

Hartenberg, R., and J. Schmidt. 1969. "The Egyptian Drill and the Origin of the Crank," *Technology and Culture* 10:155–66.

Hayes, J. W. 1972. *Late Roman Pottery.* London: British School at Rome.

*Higashi, E. L. 1990. "Conical Glass Vessels from Karanis: Function and Meaning in a Pagan/Christian Context in Rural Egypt." 2 vols. Ann Arbor: University of Michigan. Ph.D. dissertation.

Hunt, A. S. 1922. "Twenty-Five Years of Papyrology," *Journal of Egyptian Archaeology* 8:121–28.

*Hussain, A. G. 1983. "Magnetic Prospecting for Archaeology in Kom Oshim and Kiman Fares, Fayum, Egypt." *Zeitschrift für ägyptische Sprache und Altertumskunde* 110:36–51.

Husselman, E. M. 1952. "The Granaries of Karanis," *Transactions of the American Philological Society* 83:56–73.

——. 1953. "The Dovecotes of Karanis," *Transactions of the American Philological Society* 84:81–91.

——. 1958. "Report of the Supervisors of the Oil Tax," *Transactions of the American Philological Society* 89:132–37.

——. 1971. *Papyri from Karanis, Third Series (Michigan Papyri, Vol. IX).* American Philological Association Monograph 29. n.p.: American Philological Association.

——. 1979. *Karanis. Excavations of The University of Michigan in Eygpt, 1928–35: Topography and Architecture.* Kelsey Museum of Archaeology Studies 5. Ann Arbor: Kelsey Museum of Archaeology.

Johnson, A. C. 1936. *Roman Egypt.* An Economic Survey of Ancient Rome II. Baltimore: Johns Hopkins University Press.

Johnson, B. 1981. *Pottery from Karanis. Excavations of The University of Michigan.* Kelsey Museum of Archaeology Studies 7. Ann Arbor: Kelsey Museum of Archaeology.

Jones, A. H. M. 1960. "The Cloth Industry under the Roman Empire," *Economic History Review,* ser. 2, 12:183–92.

*Keenan, J. G. 2003. "Deserted Villages: From the Ancient to the Medieval Fayyum," *Bulletin of the American Society of Papyrologists* 40:119–39.

Kees, H. 1929. "Kulttopographische und mythologische Beitrage," *Zeitschrift für ägyptische Sprache und Altertumskunde* 64:99–112.

——. 1931. "Suchos," *Paulys Real-Encyclopädie,* ser. 2, vol. 4: cols. 540–60.

——. 1961. *Ancient Egypt: A Geographical History of the Nile,* ed. T. G. H. James. Chicago: University of Chicago Press.

Kelsey, F. W. 1926. University of Michigan Near East Research Committee: Memorandum 14 (unpublished manuscript, Kelsey Museum of Archaeology).

*——. 1927. "Fouilles américaines à Kom Osim (Fayum)," *Chronique d'Égypte* 5:78–79.

Kemp, B. J. 1977. "The City of El-Amarna as a Source for the Study of Urban Society in Ancient Egypt," *World Archaeology* 9:123–29.

Kuentz, M. C. 1929. "Quelques monuments de culte de Sobk," *Bulletin de l'Institut Français d'Archéologie Orientale* 28:113–72.

Leek, F. F. 1972. "Teeth and Bread in Ancient Egypt," *Journal of Egyptian Archaeology* 58:126–32.

——. 1973. "Further Studies Concerning Ancient Egyptian Bread," *Journal of Egyptian Archaeology* 59:199–204.

Lewis, N. 1967. *Greek Papyri in the Collection of New York University I: Fourth Century Documents from Karanis.* New York University Department of Classics, Monographs on Mediterranean Antiquity. Leiden: E. J. Brill.

Lindsay, J. 1963. *Daily Life in Roman Egypt.* London: F. Mullen.

Lucas, A., and J. R. Harris. 1962. *Ancient Egyptian Materials and Industries,* 4th ed. London: E. Arnold.

*Maguire, E. D., H. P. Maguire and M. J. Duncan-Flowers. 1989. *Art and Holy Powers in the Early Christian House.* Illinois Byzantine Studies 2. Urbana: University of Illinois Press. [Exhibition catalogue with Karanis objects]

Milne, J. G. 1924. *A History of Egypt under Roman Rule*, 3rd ed. London: Methuen.

*Minnen, P. van. 1994. "House-to-House Enquiries: An Interdisciplinary Approach to Roman Karanis," *Zeitschrift für Papyrologie und Epigraphik* 100:227–51.
*———. 1995. "Deserted Villages: Two Late Antique Town Sites in Egypt," *Bulletin of the American Society of Papyrologists* 32:41–56. [Discussion of the possible dates of abandonment of Karanis and Soknopaiou Nesos]

Montet, P. 1958. *Everyday Life in Egypt in the Days of Ramesses the Great.* London: E. Arnold.

*Montserrat, D. 1996. "'No Papyrus and No Portraits': Hogarth, Grenfell and the First Season in the Fayum, 1895–6," *Bulletin of the American Society of Papyrologists* 33:133–76.

Packman, Z. 1968. *The Taxes in Grain in Ptolemaic Egypt.* American Studies in Papyrology 4. New Haven: American Society of Papyrologists.

Parlasca, K. 1966, *Mumienporträts und verwandte Denkmäler* (Wiesbaden).

*Pearl, O. M. 1968. *Ptolemy, the Son of Kastor: An Egyptian Peasant's Year.* The Mary J. Pearl Lecture in Ancient Classical Culture. n.p.: Sweet Briar College. [Privately circulated printing of a lecture on a year in the life of an Egyptian farmer, based on evidence from Karanis]

Peterson, E. E. n.d. "The Architecture and Topography of Karanis" (unpublished manuscript, Kelsey Museum of Archaeology).

Petrie, W. M. F. 1890, *Kanun, Gurob, and Hawara.* London: K. Paul, Trench and Trubner.
———. 1892, *Ten Years of Digging in Egypt: 1881–1891.* London: The Religious Tract Society.
———. 1917. *Tools and Weapons.* London: British School of Archaeology in Egypt.
———. 1927. *Objects of Daily Use.* London: British School of Archaeology in Egypt.
———. 1938. *Egyptian Architecture.* London: British School of Archaeology in Egypt.

*Pollard, N. 1998. "The Chronology and Economic Condition of Late Roman Karanis: An Archaeological Reassessment," *Journal of the American Research Center in Egypt* 35:147–62.

Riad, H., and J. C. Shelton. 1975. *A Tax List from Karanis (P.Cair. Mich. 359), Part I.* Papyrologische Texte und Abhandlungen 17. Bonn: Habelt.

Richter, G. M. A. 1966. *The Furniture of the Greeks, Etruscans and Romans.* London: Phaidon.

Rickman, G. 1971. *Roman Granaries and Store Buildings.* Cambridge: Cambridge University Press.
———. 1980. *The Corn Supply of Ancient Rome.* Oxford: Clarendon Press.

Robinson, D. M., and J. W. Graham. 1938. *The Hellenic House.* Excavations at Olynthus 8. Baltimore: Johns Hopkins University Press.

Root, M. C., with the assistance of L. A. McCoy. 1982. *Wondrous Glass: Reflections on the World of Rome.* Ann Arbor: Kelsey Museum of Archaeology.

Rostovtzeff, M. 1926. *The Social and Economic History of the Roman Empire.* Oxford: Clarendon Press.
———. 1931. *The Social and Economic History of the Roman Empire*, 2nd ed. Oxford: Clarendon Press.

*Rowlandson, J., ed. 1998. *Women and Society in Greek and Roman Egypt.* Cambridge: Cambridge University Press.

Rübsam, W. J. R. 1974. *Gotter und Kulte in Faijum während der griechisch-romisch-byzantinischen Zeit.* Marburg/Lahn: E. Symon.

*Sanders, H. A., and J. E. Dunlap. 1947. *Latin Papyri in the University of Michigan Collection (Michigan Papyri, Vol. VII).* University of Michigan Studies, Humanistic Series, vol. 48. Ann Arbor: University of Michigan Press. [Includes texts from Karanis]

*Schuman, V. B. 1934. "So This is Archaeology." *Classical Journal* 29:591–98. [Anecdotal account of the University of Michigan excavation of Karanis]

Shelton, J. C. 1977. *A Tax List from Karanis (P.Cair. Mich. 359), Part II.* Papyrologische Texte und Abhandlungen 18. Bonn: Habelt.

Shier, L. 1949, "A Roman Town in Egypt," *The Classical Outlook* 26:61–63.
———. 1978, *Terracotta Lamps from Karanis, Egypt* (Ann Arbor: Kelsey Museum of Archaeology Studies 3). [Note also review by C. Grande in *Journal of Roman Studies* 75 (1985) 284, suggesting a much later date for some of the lamps]

Singer, C., et al. 1957. *A History of Technology II*. Oxford: Clarendon Press. [Including C. Aldred, "Fine Wood Work," 684–703, G. M. Crowfoot, "Textiles, Basketry, and Mats," 413–47, R. J. Forbes, "Chemical, Culinary and Cosmetic Arts," 238–98, K. R. Gibert, "Rope-Making," 451–55, J. Grant, "A Note on the Materials of Ancient Textiles and Baskets," 447–51]

*Thomas, N., ed. 1995. *The American Discovery of Egypt*. Los Angeles: Los Angeles County Art Museum. [Kelsey Museum Karanis material on pp. 227–30]

*Thomas, T. K. 2001. *Textiles from Karanis, Egypt, in the Kelsey Museum of Archaeology: Artifacts of Everyday Life*. Ann Arbor: Kelsey Museum of Archaeology.
*———. 2001–2003. "Archaeological Textiles at the Kelsey Museum: Recent Projects," *Bulletin of the University of Michigan Museums of Art and Archaeology* 14:35–40.

Toutain, J. 1915. "Le culte du crocodile dans le Fayum." *Revue d'Histoire des Religions* 71:171–94.

Turner, E. 1982. "The Graeco-Roman Branch." In: *Excavating in Egypt: The Egypt Exploration Society 1882–1982*, ed. T. G. H. James, 161–76. London: British Museum Publications.

"Unearthing the Past: The Expeditions of the Kelsey Museum." 1972. *Research News* XIII, no. 5. Ann Arbor: Office of Research Administration, The University of Michigan.

*Wagner, G., and S. A. A. El-Nassery. 1975. "Une nouvelle dédicace au grand dieu Soxis," *Zeitschrift für Papyrologie und Epigraphik* 19:139–42. [From Karanis]

Wallace, S. L. 1938. *Taxation in Egypt from Augustus to Diocletian*. Princeton University Studies in Papyrology. Princeton: Princeton University Press.

Wanscher, O. 1966. *The Art of Furniture: 5000 Years of Furniture and Interiors*. New York: Reinhold.

Wild, J. P. 1970. *Textile Manufacture in the Northern Roman Provinces*. Cambridge: Cambridge University Press.

*Wilfong, T. G. 1997. *Women and Gender in Ancient Egypt: From Prehistory to Late Antiquity*. Ann Arbor: Kelsey Museum of Archaeology.
*———. 1999. "Fayum, Graeco-Roman Sites." In: *Encyclopedia of the Archaeology of Ancient Egypt*, ed. K. A. Bard, 308–13. New York: Routledge.

Williams, C. R. 1924. *The New York Historical Society, Catalogue of Egyptian Antiquities: Gold and Silver Jewelry and Related Objects*. New York: New York Historical Society.

Wilson, L. 1933. *Ancient Textiles from Egypt in The University of Michigan Collection*. University of Michigan Studies, Humanistic Series, vol. 31. Ann Arbor: University of Michigan Press.

*Winter, J. G. 1936. *Papyri in the University of Michigan Collection: Miscellaneous Papyri (Michigan Papyri, Vol. III)*. University of Michigan Studies, Humanistic Series, vol. 40. Ann Arbor: University of Michigan Press. [Text 169 a diptych in Greek and Latin from the Karanis excavations]

Witt, R. E. 1971. *Isis in the Graeco-Roman World*. Aspects of Greek and Roman Life. Ithaca, New York: Cornell University Press.

Yeivin, S. 1934. "Notes on the Northern Temple at Karanis," *Aegyptus* 14:71–79.

Youtie, H. C. 1948. "The Kline of Sarapis," *Harvard Theological Review* 41:9–29.

*Youtie, H. C., V. B. Schuman and O. M. Pearl. 1936–39. *Tax Rolls from Karanis in Two Volumes (Michigan Papyri, Vol. IV, Part I–II)*. University of Michigan Studies, Humanistic Series, vols. 42–43. Ann Arbor: University of Michigan Press.

*Youtie, H. C. and O. M. Pearl. 1944. *Papyri and Ostraca from Karanis (Michigan Papyri, Vol. VI)*. University of Michigan Studies, Humanistic Series, vol. 47. Ann Arbor: University of Michigan Press.

Youtie, H. C., and J. G. Winter. 1951. *Papyri and Ostraca from Karanis, Second Series (Michigan Papyri, Vol. VIII)*. University of Michigan Studies, Humanistic Series, vol. 50. Ann Arbor: University of Michigan Press.